SHAKESPEARE'S
TROILUS AND CRESSIDA
& THE LEGENDS OF TROY

BY ROBERT K. PRESSON

Assistant Professor of English, University of Wisconsin

MADISON, 1953

THE UNIVERSITY OF WISCONSIN PRESS

Reprinted with permission from the edition of 1953, Madison
First AMS EDITION published 1971
Manufactured in the United States of America

International Standard Book Number: 0-404-05134-0

Library of Congress Catalog Number: 70-172506

85-1142

AMS PRESS INC.
NEW YORK, N.Y. 10003

SHAKESPEARE'S TROILUS & CRESSIDA
AND THE LEGENDS OF TROY

AMS PRESS
NEW YORK

TO MY FATHER AND MOTHER

PREFACE

In this comparative analysis of the legends of Troy Shakespeare made use of, I have limited myself to a discussion of plot, characterization, theme. I have not attempted to account for influences on form or thought not definitely discernible in the source material. In my analysis of the composition of each scene of the play, I have not refrained, however, from suggesting reasons for Shakespeare's altering the legends, or for his following one version rather than another.

It was a suggestion by Professor Douglas Bush a few years ago that prompted this investigation, but his influence did not stop there. More recently I have sought counsel from colleagues at the University of Wisconsin. Had my competence been greater, I would have incorporated more suggestions made by Professors Helen C. White, Ruth Wallerstein, Merritt Y. Hughes, Jerome H. Buckley. Also I am happily indebted to Professor G. Blakemore Evans for general and specific criticism.

Miss Sina K. Spiker and Mr. Vernon Sternberg have been most helpful and expert in preparing the manuscript for the process of photo-offset printing.

The book is in my name but my aunt, Miss Beulah King, has been in diverse ways a collaborator.

TABLE OF CONTENTS

CHAPTER I: INTRODUCTION

1. The Matter of Troy

INTRODUCTION

1. The Matter of Troy

Elizabethan poets and playwrights, editors and translators, did much to exploit their public's interest in the legends of Troy. Though familiar to readers from an early date, it was in the last years of Elizabeth's reign, particularly from 1596 to 1602, that the public interest in the Ten Years' War became most pronounced, as the number of books printed and plays produced testifies. For the most part, booksellers at St. Paul's and elsewhere, and the theatre managers on the Bankside and possibly those in the City, offered the reader and spectator what might be called traditional versions of the Trojan saga: only between 1598 and 1602 was an attempt made to introduce a "new" tradition of the Trojan War.

In 1596, Thomas Creede republished Caxton's Recuyell of the his-toryes of Troye[1] under the title of The Auncient Historie, of the des-truction of Troy, "Newly corrected, and the English much amended, by William Fiston."[2] This lengthy chronicle of the deeds of Hercules and the many incidents in the Trojan wars had been a favorite with several generations before Shakespeare's,[3] and in his time begot a dramatic progeny of dubious fame.

In the year that Creede published the Recuyell, Philip Henslowe, then owner and manager of the Rose, methodically entered in his diary the receipts for a new play called "troye."[4] The play is lost, and though the author is unknown, scholars have attempted (and it must be said on shaky evidence) to identify it as an early version of Heywood's

1. Ed. H. Oskar Sommer (London, 1894), 2 vols.
2. (London, 1596). Microfilm, Modern Language Association Reprint No. 71. I quote from the Fiston text, and in the notes abbreviate the title thus: AH. Since the Sommer text is more accessible, I give corresponding page references to that edition, and call Caxton's work the Recuyell throughout my discussion.
3. It passed through three editions from 1475 to 1553. Fiston's was the fourth. For the date of the first edition see Seymour de Ricci, A Census of Caxton, in Illustrated Monographs, No. 15, printed for the Bibliographical Society (Oxford, 1909), p. 3.
4. "ye 22 of June 1596 ne . . . R, at troye . . . iij^{li} ix^{s}."—Henslowe's Diary (ed. W. W. Greg, London, 1904), I, 42.

Iron Age.[5] "Troye" seems to have enjoyed a brief success. From the twenty-second of June until the sixteenth of July, five performances are recorded.[6] Thereafter the play is not mentioned by Henslowe. No evidence exists to indicate that this production stimulated a rival company to produce a play on the same subject.

Three years later, however, in 1599, Henslowe records payment to Dekker and Chettle for a play called "troylless & creseda."[7] The time was apparently propitious for another dramatic treatment of "The Matter of Troy," though, of course, in the 1596 "troye," there may have been no dramatization of the love of Troilus and Cressida, nor of that period of the wars when Hector and Achilles were the prime contenders. Though Dekker and Chettle's play is lost,[8] an outline of its principal scenes exists, and from it one can draw the conclusion that the form of the play was of the loose chronicle type and that the subject matter was in the main derived from Caxton or Lydgate.[9] It is evident that the authors had recourse to Chaucer's Troilus and Criseyde and to Henryson's version of the last days of Cressida since in the play her end is treated in what was a prominent scene. "Enter Cressida, wth Beggars . . . !"

Though we have no record that indicates whether or not the play was a success, the fact that the Lord Chamberlain's Company elected to produce a play on the subject is reasonable, though indirect, evidence that the Admiral play had not lost money for its producers. Presumably sometime in 1601-02, Shakespeare was engaged to write a version of the story.[10] The very existence of recent plays on "The Matter of Troy," though useful as guides, created problems in the presentation. To follow Caxton, as Dekker and Chettle seem to have done, would have been to write another Admiral play, for even though the spirit and the dialogue might be very different, a new play in the fa-

---

5. See particularly John S. P. Tatlock, "The Siege of Troy in Elizabethan Literature, Especially in Shakespeare and Heywood," PMLA, XXX (1915), 710.

6. Henslowe's Diary, I, 42.

7. Ibid., I, 109.

8. Reasonably identified as the Admiral Fragment. Ibid., II, 202.

9. Tatlock favors Lydgate.—PMLA, XXX (1915), 702, n. 13. Of course, too little of the play remains to allow one to determine precisely the source.

10. The only evidence for the date of the play is the entry in the Stationers' Register, February 7, 1603: "Master Robertes, Entred for his copie in full Court holden this day to print when he hath gotten sufficient aucthority for yt, The booke of 'Troilus and Cresseda' as yt is acted by my lord Chamberlens Men." The play was printed in 1609 in two issues. To one is prefixed the preface in which the writer mentions the play as "neuer stal'd with the Stage, neuer clapperclawd with the palmes of the vulger . . . !" I accept Lawrence's interpretation that the play was not a popular success.— William W. Lawrence, Shakespeare's Problem Comedies (New York, 1931), pp. 129-33.

miliar pattern would not offer definite prospects of success. The mediaeval[11] version was not capable of infinite variation or exploitation on the popular stage. Doubtless for such a reason, Shakespeare, for the play he was to write, turned to what might be called a "new" tradition of the story, though in reality the oldest of all: the Homeric tradition. In 1598, Chapman had published eight books of the Iliades, and thus presented the first important classical version of the story that countered the mediaeval.[12]

Between the two accounts there are great differences in the conception and treatment of characters and in narrative technique, and there are differences (equally important though less easy to summarize) in the total impression each version leaves. In Chapman's Homer, the characters are conspicuously emphasized. Their passions, and thoughts, their reactions to events, their thoughts during and after action are dwelt on. There is an emphasis on the characters of the heroes rather than on mere deeds alone. But in the mediaeval accounts the emphasis is on the activities of the heroes. Their natures are not developed; their reactions are not explored to any extent. Neither by self-revelation, nor by the authors' analyses do the characters emerge as they would were an emphasis on them rather than on the narrative.

Despite the detailed descriptions Lydgate lavishes on the personal appearances of his characters,[13] and despite the similar though less detailed accounts by Caxton, in neither translation do the characters appear more than types—types, one may add, one meets with in numerous mediaeval romances. Hector, the perfect knight, is the flower and pattern of chivalry. He could as well be met with in Winchester as in Ilium. Troilus is scarcely different as a person or knight, though his story is not the same. Paris is the courtly lover—but not the individual courtly lover Chaucer conceived of in his Troilus: Helen is the woman in the court of love but not an individual such as Criseyde. Agamemnon, Ulysses, Nestor have different experiences, of course, and different labels too, but one is not easily distinguished from another by real character. But in the epic, the heroes are very much

11. Though the ultimate origins of the Recuyell are to be traced to the works of Dares and Dictys, "mediaeval" is used to describe their versions of the Graeco–Trojan wars, since in the Middle Ages their histories became more popular and influential than Homer's.

12. Throughout this discussion reference is to the Seauen Bookes of the Iliades of Homere, translated by George Chapman (London, 1598). With it was published Achilles Shield. The seven books are I, II, VII–XI; Achilles Shield is part of Book XVIII. Arthur Hall had published the first ten books of the Iliad in 1581. There was but one edition. Shakespeare shows no knowledge of it. The translation is discussed by H. G. Wright, The Life and Works of Arthur Hall (Manchester University Press, 1919), pp. 135 ff.

13. Troy Book, II.4509 ff. (ed. Henry Bergen for the Old English Text Society, London, 1906). All references to Lydgate are to this edition.

characters. Nestor and Ulysses are individuals, as are Agamemnon and Menelaus. And Achilles is a complex figure that one does not meet with in the mediaeval accounts—save in name

It is well to remember that the characters in the mediaeval histories are essentially types, are simple in conception and forthrightly drawn, whereas the characters as they appear in the epic are individuals, are fully developed and sometimes complex in conception, since the quality of characterization in the sources influenced Shakespeare's portraiture in Troilus and Cressida.

Narrative technique is by no means the same in Lydgate and Caxton, and in Homer. The difference in handling "The Matter of Troy" is principally caused by the differences in mediums. The mediaevalists were writing chronicles of Troy: Homer, an epic. Lydgate and Caxton are concerned with the story of the city long before King Priam ruled, and long after Hector was slain. The Ten Years' War, though the most important period, is but one episode in the lengthy history of the country. One event follows another, one group of characters gives way to a second, as the narrative rapidly moves on in Caxton, and moves eddyingly on in Lydgate. The epic, of course, is no comprehensive survey of the history of Troy. One major incident, the wrath of Achilles and the effect of that on the Greeks, comprises the action of the Iliades. Numerous.incidents take place as a result of Achilles' behaviour, to be sure, but all episodes are connected with his action. Thus the epic, with its nucleus of action, is quite unlike the histories with their multiplicity of event, and lack of selection of material. Furthermore, in the mediaeval accounts there is not the build-up or heightening of individual scenes that one meets with in the Iliades; a feature which makes the epic seem, at least, more readily adaptable for dramatization—provided the dramatist is not writing in the chronicle mould.

Since each writer stresses different aspects of his subject, each narrative leaves a total impression unlike that of another, though a hasty reading of Lydgate and Caxton suggests they are as different as are mares'and horses' hoofs. Caxton in a plain, straightforward style passes from one happening to another without dramatic build-up of scenes, and without assigning to his characters more character than labels suffice for. In his account he stresses above all the activities of the heroes in the field. The general melees, and the individual combats, preoccupy the translator with the result that the total picture left by the Recuyell is one of constant and violent physical warfare.

Lydgate likewise dwells upon the activities of the knights in the field, but a didactic purpose, more discernible than in Caxton, prompts his lengthy descriptions of heroes arming, their behaviour before, during, and after combat. He wrote the Troy Book at the suggestion of Henry Bolingbroke since the Prince wished to see the famous warriors of antiquity living again as knights and practicing the principles laid down in the code of knighthood.[14] The ancients were to be the models for Henry and his lords to guide their lives by. Hence the Troy Book has the air of a conduct book with the stress placed by the author on knightly behaviour, and consequently, detailed accounts abound of what qualities make or mar knights. Hector emerges, of course, as the chivalric ideal in war, in sport, and in council.

Chapman's first translation of the Iliades is fragmentary indeed, but a composite picture grows out of the action that clearly explains why the humanist translator regarded the poem as a supreme example of "Predominant Perturbation."[15] In it is depicted a society disintegrating because of the dissension of powerful individuals whose passions are so excessive that reason cannot control them. The ninth century epic has become something of a sixteenth century humanist tract.

Shakespeare's Troilus and Cressida shows affinities with the sources it grew from. His characters, like Homer's, are individuals rather than types. They are fully developed, and are sometimes complex. They are never animated labels. In epic and play there is an emphasis on character and not on deeds alone.

Also, the play is rather closer to the epic in form since Shakespeare did not write an historical pageant, or chronicle of the entire history of Troy, but selected one period for the dramatic action—and that period when Achilles and Hector were the contenders. However, Troilus and Cressida is not without some relationship to the histories in form since Shakespeare wove into the war plot the love story of Troilus and Cressida—a suggestion prompted by them,[16] though for the incidents he used Chaucer's poem, as we shall note. But the legend of the lovers is related in the play to the war plot by a theme common to both[17]—whereas it is not in Lydgate and Caxton.

The impressions left by Troilus and Cressida are most assuredly not those of ordeal and fierce warfare, nor is the play a conduct book designed to illustrate the code of knighthood in terms of ancient "exempla." Rather the impression the play leaves is not unlike that of the incomplete Iliades as translated and interpolated by Chapman.[18] The trials and harms dissension brings to a society, and the pertur-

14. Ibid., Prologue, 73–103.
15. The Epistle Dedicatory, in The Odysseys of Homer (ed. Richard Hooper, London, 1897), I, xlvii.
16. For the love story—the episodes, dialogue, and place of conclusion —Shakespeare went to Chaucer's poem. The suggestion, though, to include their story in the war plot must have come from the mediaeval historians. This inclusion gives the play a superficial resemblance to the chronicle type, but thematically the love story is bound to the war plot. See below, p. 133. For Shakespeare's handling of the Troilus and Cressida source material, see below, pp. 107–33.
17. See below, p. 141.
18. See Phyllis B. Bartlett, "The Heroes of Chapman's Homer," RES, XVII (1941), 257–80; Donald Smalley, "Ethical Bias in Chapman's Homer," SP, XXXVI (1939).

bations passion when unbridled by reason brings to the possessor
and to his dependents are familiar humanistic ideas abundantly exemplified by the behaviour of the characters in play and poem. The
chaos that follows from judgments blinded by emotions is presented
in lively fashion by the ancient "exempla."

Critics have often sought the meaning of Troilus and Cressida[19] in
the sources—or at least have attempted to account for Shakespeare's
handling of "The Matter of Troy" by its treatment in Lydgate and
Caxton. That the mediaeval tradition played a large part in the forma-
tion of the play Professor Tillyard has most recently demonstrated,[20]
but the "new" or classical conception as understood and made available
by Chapman must not be overlooked as a major source that influenced
Shakespeare in writing Troilus and Cressida.

If it is true that Shakespeare was ready to take advantage of popu-

---

19. Other plays on "The Matter of Troy" (now lost) that appeared in
the last decade of the century are listed by Tatlock, PMLA, XXX (1915),
676–78. From their titles one gathers, justifiably, that the subject
matter was only indirectly concerned with the period of the Ten Years'
War. No mention is made above of the Welsh Troelws and Kressyd. It
appears to be of later date than Shakespeare's play. For discussion of
the date, see Tatlock, "The Welsh Troilus and Cressida, and its relation to the Elizabethan Drama," MLR, X (1915), 265 ff.

20. E. M. W. Tillyard, Shakespeare's Problem Plays (Toronto,
1949), pp. 37–49. Professor Tillyard readily dismisses Chapman's
Homer with the remark that "Troilus and Cressida need bear no
relation to those books of Chapman's Homer published in 1598. It
is true that Shakespeare was very unlikely not to have read them,
but it is equally true that the bulk of his material was medieval
and that for the small residue he need not have gone to Chapman."
The "residue" is mentioned on pages 37–38. Tillyard sees Shakespeare's debt as a heavy one to Lydgate, even as had W. B. Drayton Henderson ("Shakespeare's Troilus and Cressida," in Essays
in Dramatic Literature, Parrot Presentation Volume, ed. Hardin
Craig, Princeton, 1935, pp. 127–56). It seems to me both authors
would have considerably revised their statements had they compared the play with the Chapman translation, Lydgate, and Caxton.
But scholars have had a way of not looking into Chapman's Homer.
The neglect is a common failing. Sir Sidney Lee wrote that "Shakespeare may have read the first instalment of Chapman's great translation . . . . But the drama owed nothing to Homer's epic."—A Life
of William Shakespeare (New York, 1922), p. 371. And even more
recently E. E. Stoll observed that "it is unlikely that Shakespeare
read Homer in Greek, and likely that he did not even in translation
. . . ."—Shakespeare and Other Masters (Cambridge, 1940), p. 362.
Parrott makes a similar statement: ". . . . there is no reason whatever to believe that Shakespeare read Greek or had any acquaintance
with Greek literature—except Plutarch—either in the original or
in translation."—Thomas M. Parrott, Shakespeare's Twenty-Three
Plays and the Sonnets (New York, 1938), p. 5.

lar taste, and in a measure to cater to it, it is not surprising that about 1601-02 he should undertake a dramatic version of "The Matter of Troy" for his company, since we know that at least two plays had been produced on the general subject in a relatively short time, a prose history was enjoying success (a fifth edition of Caxton's history appeared in 1607), Chaucer's poem was newly edited in 1598 by Thomas Speght, and a recent translation of part of the Iliades was available. But it would be surprising when we consider the number of books and plays on the subject, if Shakespeare, to construct his plot, had not turned to the least exploited version of the saga at that time: Chapman's Homer.

THE SIEGE PLOT

2. Dissension in the Greek Army

SHAKESPEARE

Disintegration of their army is the concern of the Greek leaders
as they first assemble in <u>Troilus and Cressida</u>. It is the seventh
year of the siege, but the time has not yet come when Ilium's "towers,
whose wanton tops do buss the clouds, Must kiss their own feet."[1]
Dissension among the Greeks has become, as Nestor puts it, "The
fever whereof all our power is sick." The horrors of disorder—
whether in the solar system, or in the state, or, as here, in a fighting force—are eloquently stated by Ulysses.

> The heavens themselves, the planets, and
>   this centre,
> Observe degree, priority, and place,
> Insisture, course, proportion, season, form,
> Office, and custom, in all line of order:
> And therefore is the glorious planet Sol
> In noble eminence enthron'd and spher'd
> Amidst the other; whose med'cinable eye
> Corrects the ill aspects of planets evil . . . . [I.iii.85-92]

Chaos has followed Discord's seizure of the scepter and the throne.

> Take but degree away, untune that string,
> And, hark! what discord follows; each thing
> Meets in mere oppugnancy: the bounded waters
> Should lift their bosoms higher than the shores,
> And make a sop of all this solid globe:
> Strength should be lord of imbecility,
> And the rude son should strike his father dead:
> Force should be right; or rather, right and wrong,
> Between whose endless jar justice resides,
> Should lose their names, and so should justice too.
> Then every thing includes itself in power,

1. <u>Troilus and Cressida</u>, IV.v.220 ff. All references to the play
are to the Arden Edition, ed. K. Deighton (London, 1906).

13

> Power into will, will into appetite;
> And appetite, an universal wolf,
> So doubly seconded with will and power,
> Must make perforce an universal prey,
> And last eat up himself.   [I.iii.109-24]

Agamemnon, "the nerve and bone of Greece," accepts this "sickness," as one beyond his control. Dissension and failure to achieve victory are not indications of faulty leadership: they are trials placed on men by Jove to find their "persistive constancy." Only those who can endure affliction and surmount all obstacles, can attain victory.

> Why then, you princes,
> Do you with cheeks abash'd behold our works,
> And call them shames? which are indeed nought else
> But the protractive trials of great Jove
> To find persistive constancy in men:
> The fineness of which metal is not found
> In fortune's love; for then the bold and coward,
> The wise and fool, the artist and unread,
> The hard and soft, seem all affined and kin:
> But, in the wind and tempest of her frown,
> Distinction, with a broad and powerful fan,
> Puffing at all, winnows the light away . . . . [I.iii.17-28]

Such a philosophy, a mixture of fatalism and stoicism, accounts for the disadvantageous position of the army. It is not exactly the creed a leader of a successful force would espouse. It is an admirable philosophy for enduring a position: a deplorable one for creating an advantage.

Nestor expands and applies Agamemnon's words, but Ulysses does not have the same outlook. To his seeming, dissension is not caused by an intervention of Zeus to test the metal of the fighters, but by the failure of the Greek leaders to maintain unity and discipline within the army. Though Agamemnon in his opening speech had hastily and with some show of choler passed over the imputation of his incompetence, Ulysses in general and inoffensive terms, reveals to Agamemnon that his policy alone is responsible for the disintegration of the army. He has allowed powerful members of his force to get out of hand, to act as if they were kings and not subjects.

> O, when degree is shak'd
> Which is the ladder to all high designs,
> The enterprise is sick! . . . .
> Take but degree away, untune that string,
> And, hark! what discord follows . . . .
>   Great Agamemnon,
> This chaos, when degree is suffocate,
> Follows the choking.
> And this neglection of degree it is
> That by a pace goes backward, with a purpose
> It hath to climb.   [I.iii.101-29]

The Greek force, as Ulysses points out, is infected through and
through. Achilles and Patroclus, together with their soldiers, the
Myrmidons, are the major violators of the concept of degree.

>The great Achilles, whom opinion crowns
>The sinew and the forehand of our host,
>Having his ear full of his airy fame,
>Grows dainty of his worth, and in his tent
>Lies mocking our designs: with him Patroclus . . . .
>   [I.iii.142-46]

Since Achilles and Patroclus, as Nestor notes, are figures that
other warriors pattern themselves on, the dissension has become
widespread.

>And in the imitation of these twain,
>Who, as Ulysses says, opinion crowns
>With an imperial voice, many are infect.
>Ajax is grown self-will'd, and bears his head
>In such a rein, in full as proud a place
>As broad Achilles; keeps his tent like him;
>Makes factious feasts; rails on our state of war,
>Bold as an oracle . . . .   [I.iii.185-92]

The revolting warriors do not refrain from placing a charge of
cowardice on Agamemnon and his advisers since their work is a-
chieved rather in the tent than in the field. To the dissident chiefs,
greatness is alone garnered in combat and not at all in plotting a
campaign.

>They tax our policy, and call it cowardice;
>Count wisdom as no member of the war;
>Forestall prescience, and esteem no act
>But that of hand: the still and mental parts,
>That do contrive how many hands shall strike,
>When fitness call them on, and know by measure
>Of their observant toil the enemies' weight,—
>Why, this hath not a finger's dignity.
>They call this bed-work, mappery, closet-war . . . .
>   [I.iii.197-205]

While the dissension lasts, the insubordinate leaders pass their
time scorning and mocking their superiors.

>   The general's disdain'd
>By him one step below, he by the next,
>That next by him beneath; so every step,
>Exampled by the first pace that is sick
>Of his superior, grows to an envious fever
>Of pale and bloodless emulation . . . . [I.iii.129-34]

Ulysses concludes that Troy still stands not because the Trojans
are strong in combat and impossible to defeat, but because the Greeks
are weakened by a fever of dissension: "Troy in our weakness stands,
not in her strength."   [I.iii.137]

CAXTON

Shakespeare found no precedent in Caxton's Recuyell for opening the siege plot at the period he chose. Caxton was translating a history, supposedly a true history of the Trojan wars, and in a straightforward narrative manner began at the natural beginning and continued to the ultimate, tragic conclusion. Furthermore, if anyone in the audience had been familiar with Caxton's version of the story, he would have been aware that the motives the dramatist ascribed to the delay at this period of the siege were unfamiliar. He would not recall that Troy stood because discipline and order in the Greek army had deteriorated to so serious a degree that the Trojans were strong only by comparison. The Agamemnon that Caxton depicts is not conscious of any underlying weakness in his army;[2] the siege is protracted because the Trojans are equally strong combatants. Though the war is fated to last ten years, until after the death of Hector (save for truces dictated by sanitary considerations and the need of food),[3] battles are constant.

Of the strength of Troy and its defenders, and of the impossibility of victory before Hector falls, the Greek councilors are keenly aware. "And they said that as long as he [Hector] were aliue, and came to battaile against them, they might neuer vanquish the Troyans . . . ." [Rec.II.594; AH,512] Agamemnon does not minimize the hardships awaiting the Greek forces: Troy has many allies that King Priam has assembled from near-by provinces; the Trojans are above all fighting on home soil, which gives them immeasurable strategic advantages; and lastly, the city is strongly built and well fortified, doubly so, as Diomedes points out, for while the Greeks tarried to amass spoils from Tenedos, Priam was adding more stone to his already powerful citadel. [Rec.II.569; AH,490]

> Ye may well know for trueth, that they haue assembled in the city of Troy great power, for to defend them against us: and also the Citie is passing great and strong: and ye know well that they be upon their proper heritage, that is a thing that doubleth their force and strength. For ye may take example of the Crowe, that otherwise defendeth her nest against the fawcon.
> [Rec.II.557; AH,480]

2. In Caxton's version, dissension among the Greeks arises after Achilles has slain Hector. At that time, Palamedes, envious of Agamemnon's leadership, demands to be king, and by general approval is elected head of the army. But the transfer is effected without disrupting the command.—Recuyell, II.616 ff.; AH, 532. In Caxton, Achilles' revolt takes place after the death of Hector. See below, pp. 23–24. Lydgate's version in this period of the history is like Caxton's.—Troy Book, III.716–5480. Achilles' revolt also takes place after the death of Hector, and the cause is the same as in Caxton.—Troy Book, V. 551–2619.

3. Recuyell, II.551, 601; AH, 474, 518.

For the disunion among the Greeks as contributory to the stalemate in the war at the end of the seventh year, and the equal strength
of the Trojans, Shakespeare got no hint from Caxton, who accounts
for the delay, until the death of Hector, by the well-matched strength
of the contestants.

HOMER

In the opening of the Iliades, Homer shows the Greek army more
at war within itself than with the enemy. Nine years have passed, yet
Troy still stands. When obedience shall be restored in the command,
then, as Agamemnon notes, "Priams high-topt towers should stoope,
outfacing vs no more!" [p. 31] But the reign of chaos is meanwhile
complete.

The quarrel between Agamemnon and Achilles over the distribution
of spoils is the most disastrous during the war since Achilles, by
withdrawing from combat, gives the fighting edge to the Trojans,
whose great strength, increased by Jove's command, brings innumerable woes to the Argives and prolongs the Greek stalemate before
Ilium.

But Achilles is not the only dissatisfied chief in the command.
Discontent is more widespread. In a moment of weakness, many of
the leaders of the expedition, finding death and misery in place of
the honor and glory they sought, seeing Troy stand above the plain
as unapproachable as nine years before, while they suffer the plague
of Apollo [p. 6] and the decay of their ships [p. 24],are ready to strike
camp and board their vessels to leave to Priam and to his friends
the glory. [p. 25] To test what today would be called morale, or in
Chapman's phrase to make "tryall of [men's] spirites" [p. 26] or in
Shakespeare's words, to "find persistive constancy in men," Agamemnon draws, before the council of the assembled leaders of Greece,
a picture of home and sets it against the present conditions of the
siege all endure [p. 24]. So violent is the urge to return to the homeland, among princes as among the common soldiers, and to leave
Troy to those who possess it, that it necessitates the council of Hera
on Olympus and the very presence of Athene among the host to stop
a general flight [p. 25]. Agamemnon's speech

> mou'de to flight in euery minde, th'inglorious
>   multitude,
> Who heard not what in priuate court the counsell did
>   conclude.
> Th' assembly grew most turbulent, as billowes rude
>   and vast;
> . . . .
> All to the ships with showting ran, earth smoakd
>   beneath their feete,
> And mutually they made exhort to haile the crased
>   Fleete

Into the seas: pumpt and made cleane, and drew the
    stockes away,
Offering to lanch, the other Peeres could not be heard
    for stay:
A noyse confusde alongst the shore, did smite the
    golden stars,
From souldiers throates, whose harts did long to
    leaue such irksome wars . . . .   [Iliades, pp. 24-25]

Ulysses,

Who yet had not so much as toucht, his blackewel
    transomde barke,
But vexed in his hart and soule, the armies shame did
    marke,   [p. 25]

moves among the leaders in revolt, and reminds them that their duty
is to their king, and not to their wills. Subjects as kings are an ab-
surdity never sanctioned by Jove who has designed an ordered society.

. . . nor must Greekes be so irregular:
To liue as euery man may take the scepter from
    the king:
The rule of many is absurd, one Lord must leade
    the ring:
Of far resounding gouernment: one king whome
    Saturnes sonne,
Hath giuen a scepter and found lawes, to beare
    dominion.   [p. 26]

Though the rout is stopped by Ulysses, the revolt of Achilles and
the Myrmidons persists. Other warriors support their cause with
the result that the dissenting block is great enough to forestall victory. Revolt from degree is widespread, and the heroes, in imitation
of Achilles, spend their time in sports, and in scorning the work of
their superiors.

. . . his men yet pleasd their harts
With throwing of the holed stone, with hurling of
    their darts,
And shooting fairely on the shore: their horse at
    Chariots fed,
. . . .
His princes amorouse of their chiefe, walkt scorning
    here and there,
About the host and scornd to fight . . . .   [p. 42]

Achilles had himself scorned Agamemnon's role in the war, taxing
it with cowardice. He had not distinguished himself in the field, only
in the plotting of war which to Achilles lacked dignity.

. . . hart but of a Hart
That neuer with the formost troups, in fight darst
    shake thy dart

> Nor in darke ambush arme thy self, these seeme
>   too ful of death
> For they [sic] cold spirite . . . .   [p. 8]

Nestor, deploring the situation that has arisen, notes the pleasure it will bring to Troy.

> And how will Priam and his sonnes with all the
>   Ilion seed,
> Euen at their harts reioyce to heare, these
>   haynous discordes breed . . . .   [p. 9]

At present, says Agamemnon, Troy stands only because the Greeks are weak.

>   . . . but if intreated loue
> Make vs [Agamemnon and Achilles] with reunited
>   mindes, consult in one againe,
> Troy shall not in the left [sic] hir lothed pride
>   sustaine.   [p. 31]

Until the death of Hector, nondecisive combats between evenly matched forces was the explanation Caxton offered for the failure of the Greeks to compass the destruction of the enemy. The Trojans proved too well trained, too well equipped, for the Greeks to overcome them in fair fight.[4]

4. Thomas Heywood in the Iron Age (Dramatic Works of Thomas Heywood [London, 1847], Vol. III), does not dramatize the Agamemnon-Achilles quarrel, nor the general insubordination, as does Shakespeare. The revolt of Heywood's Achilles is owing to the entreaties of Hecuba whose daughter he hopes to wed (p. 310). This is an entirely different situation.
    The relationship between Shakespeare's play and Heywood's cannot be absolutely determined. Tatlock presumed that the Iron Age (1612) was the old play called "troye" for which Henslowe paid Heywood an advanced sum in 1596.—John S. P. Tatlock, "The Siege," PMLA, XXX (1915), 708 ff. Arthur M. Clark (Thomas Heywood, Oxford, 1931, pp. 63 ff.) and John Q. Adams ("Shakespeare, Heywood, and the Classics," MLN, XXXIV [1919], 337) disagreed with Tatlock's assumption. In the most recent report on the composition of the Iron Age, the author reaches the conclusion, that though Clark's position is firm, and though many incidents of the play were taken from Heywood's own Troia Britannica, the possibility remains that the Iron Age existed in some form in 1596.—Allan Holaday, "Heywood's Troia Britannica and the Ages," JEGP, XLV (1946), 430 ff.
    The Iron Age resembles Troilus in those incidents also found in the books of the Iliades Chapman published in 1598. It is likely that the Iron Age of 1596 lacked those Homeric episodes. It is not probable that Heywood in 1596 was familiar with the epic and by chance selected the episodes treated in the books Chapman was yet to publish. Unless Heywood revised "troye" after Chapman published, and before Shakespeare wrote, Heywood may be considered the borrower from Shakespeare.

Homer, on the other hand, emphasized dissension in the Greek command as the major cause of the Greek failure. Achilles alone has the skill to slay Hector, whose death can open up the gate of Troy to the besiegers. As long as Achilles refrains from combat, the Greek position is reduced to maintaining by desperate fighting little more than its foothold on the Scamandrian plain. But Achilles' insubordination is not an isolated instance. A general revolt from authority at one period of the war is widespread, and the impending rout of the Greeks, enforced by no pressure from the Trojans as at a later date, is a definite reality. But this general insubordination Homer treated as an incident, a sudden frenzy evoked by Agamemnon's desire to try the metal of his troops. The disintegration that follows his speech is immediately stopped by Hera and Athene. The Trojans learn nothing of it; and consequently, are unable to take strategic advantage.

Following Homer's lead, Shakespeare chose to dramatize that period during the siege (before the death of Hector), when dissension among the Greeks well-nigh cost them the victory. But he turned what was a mere episode in the Iliades into the dramatic situation of the siege plot. For the general dissent in Troilus and Cressida does not end abruptly as in the epic. Shakespeare built up the picture of the general insubordination principally by expanding and prolonging Homer's account of dissension, and also by stripping from it the suddenly provoked Homeric cause; namely, Agamemnon's decision to test the spirit of his troops for further fighting when odds appear against them. Even though Shakespeare retains Achilles as a key figure in the drama, as the embodiment of revolt, he removed him from the position of solitary insubordination he occupies throughout the Iliades and surrounded him with others besides the Myrmidons infected by the same disorder. In other words, Shakespeare, in working over the episode in Book II of the Iliades, retained (in addition to Achilles' particular revolt) a general revolt as germane to the theme and situation he was building up.

The chaos among the Greeks in the opening of play and poem is owing to neglect of the principles of degree.[5] Achilles, together with

5. Drayton B. Henderson (Essays, ed. Hardin Craig, pp. 142–44) thinks Ulysses' speech is indebted to passages in Troy Book since Lydgate uses the word "degree" from time to time. But in Shakespeare and Homer it is Ulysses who has this conception of "degree", and in Lydgate, when the word does occur, it is not in the situation dramatized. Shakespeare's use of this concept seems to me prompted by the similar passage in the Iliades. Of course, Chapman does not use the word "degree." But is was the word. Note its conjunction with "will" in a work Shakespeare knew. "For to couet without consideration, to passe the measure of his degree, and to let will run at randon, is the only destruction of all estates."—Mirror for Magistrates (ed. Joseph Haslewood, London, 1815), I, 3. The idea, suggested by the Iliades, may have been influenced by other authors' statements of the principle. See Paul Deutschberger, "Shakespere

those who imitate his actions, is an example of an insubordinate hero
—the warrior refractory and disobedient to the king enthroned by
Jove. Though the precise reasons for dissension are not the same in
drama and epic, the harm they do to the society at large is. Chaos in
both is the scene, and perturbation of spirit is the mood.

The opening of the Iliades—and we must always bear in mind that
we are dealing with a sixteenth century humanist's translation,[6] with
its powerful scenes showing a great force on the verge of victory
suddenly disintegrating because individual princes exert their wills
wrongly—presented a situation that was always of interest and concern to the Elizabethans. The great attention, as Spencer and Tillyard
have pointed out, that the age paid to the theory of degree as an ideal,
and the ills attendant on its neglect, is reflected in numerous plays,
histories, poems, and theological tracts.[7] The Iliades, then, since
they built up a situation, and stressed a theme that the Elizabethans
did not weary of, had a timely advantage for the dramatist that the
mediaeval accounts did not emphasize.

Furthermore, the classical version offered an advantage in staging
that the mediaeval account lacked. For dramatic presentation, a portrayal of two contestants with equal, well-matched strength has less
flexibility than the presentation of two opponents when one of them is
temporarily handicapped by a weakness that can be exploited. By por-
traying two forces, one hampered by a disease in its organization,
Shakespeare had to hand in the Iliades the nucleus of an unstable situation, an incident to build up, and a dilemma for sequent action to
work out. To dramatize the events as described by Caxton (before
the death of Hector), Shakespeare would have had little but combat
on the stage.

3. Motives for Achilles' Withdrawal

SHAKESPEARE

In Troilus and Cressida, Achilles' withdrawal from combat is
an instance of the disunity in the Greek command. According to
Ulysses, the cause of Achilles' refusal to seek combat is pride.

on Degree," Shakespeare Association Bulletin, XVII (1942), 203 ff.
Above all, see D. T. Starnes, "Shakespeare and Elyot's Governour,"
Texas Studies in English, VII (1927), 121 ff.

Since the ideas expressed by Ulysses are so central to the situation, and are suggested by the source material, I cannot see his
great speech as "rant," as Mark van Doren does, in Shakespeare
(New York, 1939), p. 203.

6. P. B. Bartlett, RES, XVII (1941), 257-69; Donald Smalley, SP,
XXXVI (1939), 169-82.

7. Theodore Spencer, Shakespeare and the Nature of Man (New
York, 1942); E. M. W. Tillyard, The Elizabethan World Picture
(London, 1943), pp. 7-15, in particular.

He is too proud to fight: too certain of his own worth to see the
advantage, the necessity, of keeping himself within that sphere,
that "degree," assigned to him. Greater than all others in his own
esteem, he has little respect for his superiors in command.

> The great Achilles, whom opinion crowns
> The sinew and the forehand of our host,
> Having his ear full of his airy fame,
> Grows dainty of his worth, and in his tent
> Lies mocking our designs . . . .   [I.iii.143-46]

At a later date, Ulysses describes his affliction as a disease.

> He is so plaguy proud that the death-tokens of it
> Cry "No recovery."   [II.iii.186-87]

Agamemnon's personal visit to Achilles to entreat him to return
to the field meets with no success. Agamemnon has to speak his
blunt words to Patroclus:

> Go and tell him,
> We come to speak with him; and you shall not sin
> If you do say we think him over-proud
> And under-honest, in self-assumption greater
> Than in the note of judgment . . . .   [II.iii.128-32]

What Achilles has done to warrant such pride in himself, Shakespeare does not indicate in any dramatic incident. We feel, as Ajax
does, that his behaviour is not justified by his deeds:

> Yes, lion-sick, sick of proud heart: you may call it melan-
> choly if you will favour the man;,but, by my head, 'tis pride:
> but why, why? let him show us a cause.   [II.iii.93-96]

It is not until well on in the action of the play that a second
reason for Achilles' withdrawal is introduced. Failing to arouse
him to deeds with the bait of fame, Ulysses divulges Achilles'
supposed secret, hoping thusly to win back his support by making
clear to him the shame of a passion that allows him to forget his
honor and duty.

> Achil.   Of this my privacy
> I have strong reasons.
> Ulyss.   But 'gainst your privacy
> The reasons are more potent and heroical.
> 'Tis known, Achilles, that you are in love
> With one of Priam's daughters.   [III.iii.190-94]

Patroclus is under the impression that he is responsible for
softening Achilles' desire for combat:

> To this effect, Achilles, have I mov'd you.
> A woman impudent and mannish grown
> Is not more loath'd than an effeminate man
> In time of action. I stand condemn'd for this:
> They think my little stomach to the war
> And your great love to me restrains you thus.
>   [III.iii.217-22]

Pride in himself and disdain for his superiors, love for Polyxena, and affection for Patroclus are the motives for Achilles' secession from battle in Troilus and Cressida.

CAXTON

In the version of the Trojan war that Caxton translated, Achilles is twice out of the combat. The first time he withdraws from the field he is suffering from wounds sustained in combat, the second time from wounds inflicted by Cupid.

The day the Greeks beached their ships, some unsuccessfully [Rec. II.570; AH, 481], on the Trojan coast before the city of Troy, the "bataylle mortall" began which by nightfall left the Greeks in possession of an area large enough to set up camp, although those that "had no tentes nor pauilions, lodged then vnder the leaues, the best wise that they could" [Rec. II.575; AH, 595]. During this first battle on the shore Achilles was so sorely wounded that he was unable to participate in the second battle.

> . . . the King Agamemnon . . . put in the first battel Patroclus with his people, & with them the folke of Achilles, which was not that day in the battel, for his wounds that he had, and did stay to heale them in his tent.   [Rec. II.578-79; AH, 498-99]

By the end of the first truce, which lasted two months [Rec. II. 590; AH, 509], Achilles, his wounds healed, is ready to take the field again, for the beginning of the third battle. Hector outfights Achilles in this combat and unhorses him twice.

For no other reason does Achilles absent himself from action until after the death of Hector. On the anniversary [Rec. II.618; AH, 533] of his death, Achilles, visiting the sepulchre of Hector, was "shot with the dart of loue, that stroke him to the heart so maruellously that he could not cease to behold her [Polyxena], and the more he behelde her, the more he desired her. He was so besotted on her, that he thought on no other thing, but abode in the temple vnto the euening . . . ." [Rec. II.621; AH, 538].

This was the cause and beginning of a mischief that reduced Achilles to inactivity and even led him to plead for peace between the Greeks and Trojans.

". . . it ought to suffise to us that we haue nowe slaine Hector and many other of their nobles, by the which we might now returne with our honour and worship" [Rec. II.625; AH, 538]. Since the council is not of the same mind, Achilles "commaunded his Mirmydones that they shoulde not arme them any more against the Trojans, & that they shoulde giue no counsalle nor aide vnto the Greeks" [Rec. II. 625; AH, 538].

Though Hector is dead, Troilus proves himself a not unworthy successor in fighting skill to his brother. Once more the battles become sharp and deadly. Achilles refuses to take the field though he sends to Agamemnon his Myrmidons. Their failure to stem the Trojan advances and to escape slaughter inclines Achilles to think

more of his men than of his vow to Queen Hecuba that he would
never assist the Greeks again. He returns to the battle to slay the
last stout defender of Troy.

HOMER

Wounded pride is the cause of Achilles' withdrawal in the Iliades.
To discover the cause of the plague decimating the army, Achilles
summons the Greek council. Calchas, the seer, who is reluctant to
reveal the truth until he receives assurance of protection from A-
chilles, reveals that to pacify Apollo, whose plague is afflicting the
Greeks, Agamemnon must return Chryseis to her father, a favored
priest of the god. Agamemnon swears to do so, but also vows to find
compensation for his loss in the booty of others. He reminds the
Greek leaders assembled in council that he has the authority to
plunder anyone's treasure.

> Wouldst thou thy selfe [Achilles] inioy thy prise,
>   and I sit dispossest?
> Then let the Greekes apply themselues, as much ·
>   to my request
> And with some other fit amendes my satisfac-
>   tion make,
> It not, Ile make mine owne amendes, and come
>   my selfe and take
> Thyne Aiax or Vlisses prise (men of most excellence
> And most admitted to thy loue) and let him take
>   offence.   [Iliades, pp. 5-6]

Since Agamemnon lights on Achilles' treasure, the Myrmidon
leader charges Agamemnon with failure as a great and perfect
leader. He is no true king but a "souldier-eating king" [p. 9] mindful
of no other good than his own [p. 5], rewarding deserts with neither
honor nor care [pp. 6-7], covetous past all measure of the booty of
others [p. 6]. "... it becomes not kings to tempt by wicked presi-
dent" [p. 27].
Nestor fails to pacify Achilles:

> . . . though better borne thou bee
> Because a goddesse brought thee foorth: yet
>   better man is he
> Since his command exceedes so much . . . .   [p. 10]

But Achilles, his honor touched, his pride wounded before the assembled leaders of the expedition, withdraws from an active part in
the war. His worth will become known, however, when innumerable
woes fall upon the Greeks once warfare is resumed.

> But when the vniuersall hoast shall faint with
>   strong desire
> Of wrongd Achilles, though thou pyne, thou neuer
>   shall aspyre.

> Helpe to their miseries from me, when vnderneath
>   the hand
> Of bloody Hector, cold as death their bodies spred
>   the sand,
> And thou with inwarde hands of griefe, shalt teare
>   thy desperate minde
> That to the most kinde-worthie Greeke thou wert
>   so most vnkinde.   [p. 9]

Achilles, in the council scene and also throughout the action described in the books Chapman translated, is an exemplum of excessive pride and contention. Agamemnon is incapable of dealing with either.

> Thou still art bittrest to my rule, contention and
>   sterne flight
> To thee, are unitie and peace . . . .   [p. 7]

Agamemnon contends that his seizure of Achilles' prize is to teach him a lesson, so that his

> pride may sweare
> Atrides is thy better far, and all the rest may feare
> To vaunt equallitie with mee, or take ambitious hart,
> To stand with insolence comparde, in any aduerse part.
>   [p. 7]

Such words set up strife in Achilles. Passions and Reason struggle for domination.

> This set Peleides soule on fire, and in his brisled brest
> His rationall and agrie parts, a doutfull strife possest,
> If he should draw his wreakefull sworde
> . . . .
> Or else restraine his forward mind, and calm his angers
>   heat.   [p. 7]

Athene suddenly appears to decide his conflict. "I am come t'appease Thy violent furie." [p. 8]

Achilles sheathes his sword but vows vengeance in the form of secession.

After the quarrel, Achilles is depicted as a great figure consumed by passion.[1]

___

1. Compare Clermont d'Ambois' description of Achilles in The Revenge of Bussy d'Ambois, III.iv.14–25 (Plays and Poems of George Chapman, ed. Thomas Parrot, London, 1910):

> When Homer made Achilles passionate,
> Wrathful, revengeful, and insatiate
> In his affections, what man will deny
> He did compose it all of industry,
> To let men see that men of most renown,
> Strong'st, noblest, fairest, if they set
>   not down
> Decrees within them, for disposing these,

> But Peleus sonne at his blacke fleete, sat gyrt in
>   Angers flame,
> Nor to Consults, that makes men wise; nor forth
>   to battaill came,
> But did consume his mightie heart in desolate
>   desires . . . .   [p. 16]

The Embassy, whose purpose is to sue Achilles to return to combat, fails because there is something excessive in his pride.

> Prowd wrath within hin [sic], . . . will not be implorde.
>   [p. 93]

Agamemnon eagerly asks of the returning legates

> Will he defend vs, or not yet will his prowde stomacke
>   downe?   [p. 95]

Diomedes laments to Agamemnon that the mission was sent in the first place.

> Would God Atrides thy request were yet to vndertake;
> And all thy gifts vnoffered; hees prowde enough beside:
> But this ambassage thou hast sent, will make him
>   burst with pride.   [p. 95]

Achilles' secession is an occurrence common to all the versions of the siege of Troy given by Homer, Lydgate,[2] Caxton, Shakespeare, and Heywood,[3] but the treatment of it, and the implication of it are not the same. In the Troy Book, the Recuyell, and the Iron Age (all of which are chronicles, regardless of their literary form), it is treated as an episode: in the Iliades it is the situation, the crux of following action; and in Troilus and Cressida it is the situation of the war plot.

Nor are the motives for Achilles' withdrawal the same in all accounts. Shakespeare emphasizes his pride as the primary reason for his withdrawal from action. His pride, excessive, unreasonable, will not allow him to function in the sphere assigned to him in the command. His individual exploits place him outside the pale of the "specialty of rule." Shakespeare, of course, found ample evidence for pride as an important element in Achilles' character in Chapman's translation of Homer. As characterized by Caxton, Lydgate,

---

> Of judgment, resolution, uprightness,
> And certain knowledge of their use and
>   ends,
> Mishap and misery no less extends
> To their destruction, with all that they
>   priz'd,
> Than to the poorest, and the most despis'd.

2. Troy Book, III.585, through IV.2756.

3. Heywood only writes of the withdrawal caused by Achilles' love for Polyxena. He obeys Hecuba's wishes that he stay out of combat. —Dramatic Works, III.310 ff.

and Heywood, on the other hand, Achilles is either too much occu-
pied in combat or too much engaged with Polyxena to be proud. Before
Hector is slain, he manifests no symptoms of pride. After Hector
is killed, he is a lowly, tormented lover.

However, in handling Achilles' withdrawal Shakespeare cancelled
the dramatic, Homeric cause of his secession (namely, Agamemnon's
high-handed treatment of the Myrmidon leader). The result is curious
but surely contrived. It was obviously not to Shakespeare's purpose
to write of the quarrel between Achilles and Agamemnon. It was not
even to his purpose to take account of it. And it was not simply
because he was not dramatizing the Iliades. In this instance, Shakespeare's conception of Achilles demanded a break with the Homeric
tradition. To have shown Achilles' secession as arising from the
ill-treatment he received from Agamemnon would have made his
withdrawal entirely justified, and it would not have been an instance
of the disintegrated spirit the dramatist should show to be consonant
with the theme he was developing. Achilles rightfully withdrawn in
seclusion as a result of an unjust act on the part of his superior,
and perpetrated before the assembled council, was not the kind of
hero Shakespeare wanted. It was not the right of Achilles' purpose
but the weaknesses in his character that he needed to build up—
hence his cancellation of the Homeric situation, and his dwelling
on the passion of pride as the prime cause of his rebelliousness
and disorder.

In all probability the Recuyell was the source Shakespeare used
for treating Achilles' love for Polyxena. At first sight, the transfer
of this incident to Troilus and Cressida seems no inspiration, since
Shakespeare had already given a motive for Achilles' withdrawal.
It looks like a concession to tradition,[4] or it is an example of that
haziness of motivation for which Shakespeare has sometimes been
criticized.[5] Actually, the incident, though possibly not the handling
of it, has its place in the story. It further emphasizes the degeneration that has overcome Achilles. Not only is his excessive pride
destroying the army as a whole, and rendering him well incapable
of expressing what greatness he possesses, but passion of another
kind further confuses the Myrmidon chief. How he has fallen from
greatness the addition of this episode indicates since we now see
he is willing to lose all for the love of the daughter of the enemy.

Actually the extent of the decline is further stressed by Shakespeare's addition of a third reason for Achilles' continued lethargy,
and disinterest in the campaign. His affection for Patroclus makes
him averse to action. Such a motive for Achilles' continued secession is Shakespeare's own, though the affection of Achilles for

4. Theodore Spencer, "A Commentary on Shakespeare's Troilus
and Cressida," Studies in English Literature, Tokyo, XVI (1936), 34.
5. Levin L. Schücking, Character Problems in Shakespeare's
Plays (London, 1922), pp. 226 ff.

Patroclus is obvious in the eighteenth book of the Iliades.[6] As
treated in Troilus and Cressida, however, it is a definite reason
for Achilles' refusal to fight. By this addition, Shakespeare has
piled upon Pelion Ossa to portray a lofty figure whose passions have
brought him to utter confusion. He even confesses to Ulysses:

> My mind is troubled, like a fountain stirr'd;
> And I myself see not the bottom of it.   [III.iii.315-16]

This Achilles, then, with judgment so blind that he cannot see his
true position in the army, nor see himself clearly—passion so darkens
his vision—is and is not Homer's Achilles. The heroic figure of the
ninth century B. C. has become through the translation, and in Shakespeare's intensification and elaboration of aspects of his character
revealed in that translation, a seventeenth century exemplum of
passion overcoming reason.

4. Hector's Challenge

SHAKESPEARE

After Ulysses in council has described the effect and analyzed
the cause of the weakness in the Greek army, Aeneas, as ambas-
sador, comes from Troy to the Greeks with a challenge. Hector,
who has grown rusty during the truce, sends by his emissary a
challenge to test by trial of arms his vow that his lady is the fairest, truest of all possessed by warriors.

> We have, great Agamemnon, here in Troy
> A prince call'd Hector, Priam is his father,
> Who in this dull and long-continued truce
> Is rusty grown: he bade me take a trumpet,
> And to this purpose speak: Kings, princes, lords!
> If there be one among the fair'st of Greece,
> That holds his honour higher than his ease,
> That seeks his praise more than he fears his peril,
> That knows his valour, and knows not his fear,
> That loves his mistress more than in confession,
> With truant vows to her own lips he loves,
> And dare avow her beauty and her worth
> In other arms than hers, — to him this challenge.
> Hector, in view of Trojans and of Greeks,
> Shall make it good, or do his best to do it,
> He hath a lady, wiser, fairer, truer,
> Than ever Greek did compass in his arms;
> And will to-morrow with his trumpet call
> Midway between your tents and walls of Troy,
> To rouse a Grecian that is true in love: . . . [I.iii.259–78]

6. Also mentioned by the mediaevalist: Troy Book, II.604 ff.; Recuyell, II.579, 602; AH, 499, 519.

The challenge is directed against Achilles. Nestor sees no other that the Greeks can choose to oppose Hector if they are to come off with honor. Ulysses, the most discerning of the councilors, disapproves [I.iii.356 ff.]. If Achilles defeats Hector, his already overweening pride will overbulk them all: if he is defeated by Hector, all the Greeks will suffer loss of honor [I.iii.366 ff.]. The ulterior advantage that Ulysses sees in the challenge then will have been neglected. His stratagem is to elect Ajax by lottery, and to build up his position in the host as the better man [I.iii.373-84]. Opinion, which is not stable, will pass Achilles by and blunt his pride. To regain his position, he will rouse himself to action.

CAXTON

In the Recuyell, there is no situation comparable to that which Shakespeare developed in Troilus and Cressida. The challenge Hector proposes to Achilles is not for love: there is no stratagem devised by Ulysses to drive Achilles to action.

During one of the frequent truces, Hector visits the Grecian camp, and goes to Achilles' tent. Each laments the loss of blood both sides have spilt. To forestall further slaughter, Hector and Achilles agree to a single combat which will determine the fate of Troy. This proposed combat is, however, a bargain rather than a challenge.[1]

> And if thou thinke that thou bee so strong, that thou maiest defend thee against mee, make it so that all the barons of thine hoste promise and accord that wee fight body against body, and if it happen that thou vanquish me, that my friendes and I shalbe banished out of this realme, and we shall leaue it vnto the Greekes, and thereof I shall leaue good pledge. And heerin thou maiest profite to many other, that may run in great danger, if they haunt the battaile: and if it happen that I vanquishe thee, make that all they of thy hoste depart hence, and suffer vs to liue in peace. Achilles chafed sore with these wordes, and offered him to fight this battaile, and gaue to Hector his gage, which Hector tooke and receiued gladly.   [Rec. II.603; AH, 520; Troy Book, III, 2036 ff.]

HEYWOOD

Hector's challenge in the Iron Age is closer to Shakespeare's than is either Caxton's or Lydgate's. In the Iron Age, Hector steps between the Greek and Trojan armies as they are about to join battle, and challenges to personal combat any warrior who can match his own skill in arms:

> Heare mee you warlike Greekes, you see these fields
> Are all dyde purple with the reeking gore
> Of men on both sides slaine, you see my sword

---

1. For the combat between Ajax and Hector, and its significance in relation to Shakespeare's account, see below, pp. 43-50.

Glaz'd in the sanguine moysture of your friends.
I call the sonne of Saturne for a witnesse
To Hectors words, I haue not met one Grecian
Was able to withstand mee, my strong spirit
Would faine be equal'd; Is there in your Troupes
A Knight,whose brest includes so much of valour
To meet with Hector in a single warre ?
By Ioue I thinke there is not: If there be ?
To Him I make this proffer; if the gods
Shall grant to him the honour of the day,
And I be slaine; his bee mine honoured Armes,
To hang for an eternall Monument
Of his great valour, but my mangled body
Send backe to Troy, to a red funerall pile.
But if hee fall ? the armour which hee weares
I'le lodge as Trophies on Apolloes shrine,
And yeeld his body to haue funerall rights.
And a faire Monument so neere the Sea,
That Merchants flying in their sayle-wing'd ships
Neere to the shoare in after times may say,
There lies the man Hector of Troy did slay,
And there's my Gantler to make good my challenge.

[Dramatic Works, III. 296]

There is a general reluctance among the Greeks present to touch
the gage until Achilles, who seems the obvious choice, takes action.
When he dares any one else to touch the glove, a fight between him
and Ajax who takes his dare threatens. To prevent it, Ulysses proposes that lots be marked and cast to determine Hector's opponent.
Ajax's name is on the upturned ballot.

To end this difference, and prouide a Champion
To answere Hectors honourable challenge
Of nine the most reputed valiant:
Let seuerall Lots be cast into an Helme,
Amongst them all one prise, he to whome Fortune
Shall giue the honour: let him straight be arm'd
To incounter mighty Hector on this plaine.   [III. 297]

HOMER

During a fierce combat between the Greek and Trojan armies,
Athene and Apollo meet "at Ioues broad beech," and from their
lofty position look down upon the broils below. Though Athene gives
martial strength to the Greeks and Apollo to the Trojans, both agree
to stop the burning contention for one day.

. . . yet now let me [Apollo] perswade,
This day permit not generall wounds may either side
     inuade.
Hereafter till the end of Troy they shall apply the
     fight,
Since your immortall wils resolue, to ouerturne it
     quight!   [Iliades, p. 47]

Athene favors the proposal, and the two gods determine the best
way to stop the general fighting.

> . . we will direct the spirit, that burnes in Hectors
>   brest,
> To challenge any Greeke to wounds, with single powers
>   imprest:
> Which Greekes admiring will accept, and make some one
>   stand out,
> T'encounter so diuine a foe, with a conceipt as stout. [p. 47]

Hector, on receiving this divine intelligence from Helenus, confronts the hosts and delivers his challenge.

> Heare Troians and ye well armed Greekes, what my
>   strong mind diffusde,
> Through all my spirits, commaundes me speake . . .
> Since then, the Generall Peeres of Greece, in reach
>   of one voice meete:
> Amongst you all whose brest includes, the most impul-
>   siue minde,
> Let him stand forth as combattant, by all the rest
>   designde:
> This I propose and call high Ioue, to witnesse of
>   our strife
> If he with home-thrust Iron, can reach, th' exposure
>   of my life
> (Spoyling my armes) let him at will conuey them to
>   his tent;
> But let my bodie be returnd, that Troys two-sixt
>   descent
> May waste it in the funerall Pyle; if I can slaughter
>   him,
> . . . .
> And beare his armes to Ilion, where in Apollos
>   shryne
> Ile hang them, as my trophies due: his bodie Ile
>   resigne
> To be disposed by his friends in flamie funerals,
> And honored with erected tombe; where Hellespontus
>   fals
> Into Egæum . . . .   [p. 48]

Silence follows Hector's challenge. From fear, no one dares to
take it up. But Nestor, by narrating the glorious deeds achieved by
warriors in the past when he was in his prime, stimulates the Greek
heroes to emulation. The "nine royall princes" rise to accept the
challenge [p. 51]. To decide the antagonist Nestor proposes that lots
be drawn.

> . . . let lots be drawne by all,
> His hand shall helpe the well-armd Greekes on whome
>   the lot doth fall,
> And to his wish shal he be helpt, if he escape with
>   life,

> The harmefull danger breathing fit, of this
>   aduentrous strife.   [p. 51]

That the incident of Hector's challenge in <u>Troilus and Cressida</u>
as Shakespeare treated it has original elements is obvious from a
close comparison of that incident in the several accounts examined.
In the <u>Recuyell</u>, Caxton develops an entirely different situation.
Hector makes no chivalrous challenge. He makes a bargain, even
though the gage does ratify it. What Achilles and Hector undertake
is no sportive trial by arms to test their skill in combat, but a
fight to the death to determine the fate of Troy. A humanitarian consideration that both Achilles and Hector show for their fellow
soldiers is the reason for their agreement. It will prevent further
bloodshed.

Since Achilles is still in active combat during this stage of the
siege, there is no need for Ulysses to devise a stratagem to arouse
him to action.

In the <u>Iron Age</u> the reason for the challenge is that Hector is unable in the press and throng of conflicting armies to find a warrior
who can match him in strength of arms. To find one, if he exists,
he stops the general fighting. Furthermore, Hector has no emissary
to announce his intentions. He proclaims the purpose of his challenge.
It is not a mere trial by arms. It is a fight to the finish, with the
conditions fully outlined as to the disposition of his body should he
fail to win, and the disposition of the enemy's forces should their
opponent fall.

As in the <u>Recuyell</u>, Achilles is in combat at the time Hector proposes his challenge. When Achilles finally picks up the gauntlet
after he has dared the nine most worthy to do so, Ulysses calls for
a lottery in order that the election of the Greek hero may be un-
biased. It is, by the way, an honest lottery.

In the <u>Iliades</u>, the purpose of the challenge is to stop the bloodshed among the engaged armies for one day.

>   . . . yet now let me [Apollo] perswade,
>   This day permit not generall wounds may either
>   side inuade.   [p. 47]

In his challenge Hector speaks as if the combat were to be a mortal
one: the issue of the duel is to decide the fate of Troy. He describes
what disposition is to be made of his body if he is slain, and demands
that the opponent honor his terms. Hector, of course, should have
known that the combat would not prove so serious, at least to him.
Helenus, speaking under divine sanction, makes it clear to Hector
that he will not die in this action.

>   I promise thee that yet thy soule shall not descend
>   to fates,
>   So hearde I thy suruiual cast, by the celestiall
>   states.   [p. 47]

Apollo does not intend the combat to be fatal to either side. There will be some blood, but no death. ". . . we will direct the spirit, that burnes in Hectors brest, To challenge any Greeke to wounds" [p. 47].

At this period during the siege in the Iliades, it will be recalled that Achilles is out of the fighting. Aside from Nestor's lament that he is not present to undertake the contest [pp. 49-50], there is no suggestion that any one of the Greek leaders sees in this incident an opportunity to rouse Achilles to action.

To determine Hector's opponent, it is Nestor who proposes a lottery [p. 51].

Shakespeare's situation is most certainly borrowed from Homer. That Shakespeare drew situations from Books I and II of the Iliades has been shown in Sections 2 and 3 of this study. Book VII of the Iliades immediately follows Book II, and it contains the challenge that Shakespeare adapted for Troilus and Cressida. Though the three writers under discussion made use of the challenge and the lottery, Homer and Shakespeare consider the combat as a trial in arms, a sportive contest, rather than as a fight to determine the fate of Troy. Furthermore, the incident as dramatized by Shakespeare has the same position in the general frame of the siege that it has in the Iliades: it takes place during Achilles' withdrawal. The curious transfer to Ulysses of Nestor's speech calling for a lottery is found in Heywood and in Shakespeare. The reason for the transfer in the Iron Age is that there is no Nestor in that play. In Troilus and Cressida, the reason for the transfer is no less obvious: Ulysses, the backbone of the Greeks, is the contriver of the stratagem. Nestor, in Shakespeare's play, has few ideas other than recollections of great things past. He echoes Agamemnon [I.iii.31-53]; he follows Ulysses' advice [I.iii.387-90]. He does not mould opinion and form policy as he does in the Iliades.

One sees, then, that, in respect to the time and to the place of the challenge in the action, Shakespeare's version of the challenge is closer to Homer's than to Heywood's. But Shakespeare made some additions. The chivalrous motive for the challenge is not found in any account of the siege of Troy.[2] The stratagem Ulysses devises to turn the innocent trial by arms to good account by stimulating Achilles to action is Shakespeare's conception, like the "manipulation" of the lottery.

Though Shakespeare doubtless took the challenge from the Iliades, interestingly enough, he separated it in time from the actual combat. And for a good reason. With the exception of the general fighting in the last act, there is little action in Troilus and Cressida. What

2. For a discussion of challenges that occur in literature outside the recognized sources, and in particular that occurred in Shakespeare's time, see W. W. Lawrence, Shakespeare's Problem Comedies (New York, 1931), pp. 143-45.

there is of it in the siege plot is confined to the combat between
Ajax and Hector. The play as a whole is static in nature. Action is
confined to an impression of action rather than to action itself. Had
the fight immediately followed the challenge in the first act, the
episode would hardly have been different from what it was in the
epic. It would have been a quickly begun and quickly ended episode.
But by separating the challenge from the combat, by allowing the
challenge to be delivered in Act I and the conclusion to be reached
at the end of Act IV, Shakespeare not only expanded the episode into
the main situation of the siege plot, but was also thereby able to
arouse suspense.

Since Shakespeare was converting, by separating in time, the
challenge and the combat into the main situation of his subplot, he
had to build up the challenge into a dramatic scene. In the Iron Age
and Iliades, the contest is one incident out of many in the history
of the war. No foreshadowing is demanded. But the importance of
the combat was to assume in the siege plot dictated for the dramatist a change in its presentation. So important an action required
more than a hasty presentation. As in all Shakespearean drama, a
vital action is not suddenly presented.[3] It is foreshadowed by sufficient exposition. The build up of the challenge, since it has so
definite a function in the story, is in accord with principles of Shakespearean dramatic technique.[4]

If the challenge, then, has been built up by Shakespeare to arouse
interest by a promised action, the stratagem is to maintain and
carry suspense throughout the body of the play until the combat
takes place. Its foremost purpose, of course, is to tear down Achilles'
pride by raising Ajax to an eminent position in the host. He will be
given allowance as the better man. If Achilles is to regain his lost
renown, he will have to rouse himself from his lethargy and fight
for it. Ajax must be elected if the stratagem is to succeed. Hence
the need for arranging the lottery.

An impression of action is of course greatly strengthened by this
stratagem, since in Ulysses' manipulation of it, the spectator is
more aware that something might happen than he is conscious that
nothing actually does. But Ulysses' plan was, furthermore, a uni-

3. E. E. Stoll, Shakespeare and Other Masters (Cambridge, 1940),
pp. 11 ff.
4. The reason Shakespeare chose a chivalrous motive for the
challenge is uncertain. He found no suggestion in the versions of
the siege he was familiar with. Historical precedent is no evidence
in this instance. The motive is, however, an example of that con-
tinual association of war and women, which, though traditional,
is so conspicuous in Troilus and Cressida. If Shakespeare had a
conception of the Trojans as a singularly chivalrous people, the
association in his mind of a challenge with the traditional love
motive might be spontaneous.

fying device. It makes the challenge and combat (which it is tied
into) relevant to Achilles' position in the action. Achilles, though
he does not become one of the contestants, as Ulysses had hoped
he would, nevertheless remains throughout the course of the incident the real subject of it.

5. The Embassy to Achilles

SHAKESPEARE

The visit of the Greek councilors to Achilles in an endeavor to
win him back to the field by persuasion is an incident in all the versions of the siege of Troy under consideration. In Troilus and Cressida, Agamemnon and his staff visit Achilles twice. The first time,
he refuses to "Untent his person and share the air" [II.iii.177] with
the embassy. Though he consents to see Ulysses, he cannot be persuaded "to the field to-morrow."
> . . . imagin'd worth
> Holds in his blood such swoln and hot discourse,
> That 'twixt his mental and his active parts
> Kingdom'd Achilles in commotion rages
> And batters down himself . . . .   [II.iii.181–85]

Agamemnon, loath to yield to his inferior in command, suggests
that Ajax go to him. He might succeed where the councilors fail.

> Let Ajax go to him.
> Dear lord, go you and greet him in his tent:
> 'Tis said he holds you well, and will be led
> At your request a little from himself.   [II.iii.187–90]

Ulysses immediately quashes this suggestion. To send so great
a warrior on such a mission "were to enlarge his [Achilles'] fat-
already pride" [II.iii.204], and to lower in esteem so strong a man
as "sinewy Ajax."

At this point in the action, and throughout the remainder of the
scene, Ulysses, against the background of Achilles' present beha-
vior, proceeds to execute his plan of building up Ajax, in the presence
of the general staff, as the "better man." The growing pride of Ajax,
in Nestor's words, will be the bone between the two that will "tarre
the mastiffs on" [I.iii.391]. Act II, scene iii, though an embassy
scene, is primarily a dramatic presentation of the working of Ulysses'
stratagem.

In the second meeting with Achilles, the Greek councilors behave
quite differently, though according to a pre-arranged plan. In hopes
of lowering his pride, they pass him by, or at most exchange plati-
tudes with him as he idles before his tent [III.iii.39–70]. Ulysses
remains behind.
> 'Tis like he'll question me
> Why such unplausive eyes are bent on him:
> If so, I have derision medicinable

> To use between your strangeness and his pride,
> Which his own will shall have desire to drink.
> It may do good . . . .   [III.iii.42−47]

   The "derision medicinable" is a long exposition of the instability
of personal fame and renown of one man when many are in compe-
tition. The individual, however great his past deeds may have been,
cannot live long in idleness and expect his glory to retain its luster.
Achilles has lost the esteem he had. It belongs to Ajax now. To stir
Achilles to action, by rousing in him envy for the present position
Ajax holds as chief opponent to Hector, Ulysses extols the good fortune of his rival.

> Heavens, what a man is there! a very horse;
> That has he knows not what. Nature, what things
>   there are,
> Most abject in regard, and dear in use!
> What things, again most dear in the esteem,
> And poor in worth! Now shall we see tomorrow,—
> An act that very chance doth throw upon him,—
> Ajax renown'd. O heavens! what some men do,
> While some men leave to do.
> How some men creep in skittish fortune's hall,
> Whiles others play the idiots in her eyes!
> How one man eats into another's pride,
> While pride is fasting in his wantoness!
> To see these Grecian lords! why, even already
> They clap the lubber Ajax on the shoulder
> As if his foot were on brave Hector's breast,
> And great Troy shrieking.   [III.iii.126−41]

Towards the close of the scene, Ulysses' appeal is more direct.

> The present eye praises the present object:
> Then marvel not, thou great and complete man,
> That all the Greeks begin to worship Ajax;
> Since things in motion sooner catch the eye
> Than what not stirs. The cry went once on thee,
> And still it might, and yet it may again,
> If thou would'st not entomb thyself alive,
> And case thy reputation in thy tent . . . .[III.iii.180−87]

   It is then that Achilles is shaken to confess to having strong reasons for his privacy; his love for Polyxena, which, however, has
been known to the Greek staff. Ulysses leaves Achilles with keen-
edged words most apt to bring such a man to realization of his
true position.

> But it must grieve young Pyrrhus now at home,
> When fame shall in our islands sound her trump,
> And all the Greekish girls shall tripping sing,
> "Great Hector's sister did Achilles win,
> But our great Ajax bravely beat down him."
> Farewell, my lord . . . .   [III.iii.210−15]

The purpose of the embassy has failed, but there is something more of thoughtfulness than pride in the Achilles Ulysses leaves.

CAXTON

During a two-month truce in the siege, after Hector has been slain, and while Achilles sulks in his tent for love of Polyxena, Agamemnon sends Nestor, Ulysses, and Diomedes to Achilles to beg him to return to the host to defend it against the Trojans who, though Hector is dead, are doing marvels under Troilus' direction. On this occasion, Achilles receives the ambassadors with great joy, but in spite of prayers, admonishments, and remindings that he was once most eager to leave Greece and to fight Priam and destroy his city, the leader of the Myrmidons remains in obdurate seclusion.

> . . . and we were now in hope to haue vanquished them, after that ye by your force and valour haue slaine Hector, that was the true defender of the Troyans: and also now that Deiphebus is dead, the Troyans be therewith put vnder foot, and after this day when ye haue gotten with great trauell to great worship and so good renowme, will ye nowe loose all at once, and suffer your people to be slain cruelly, that ye haue so long defended with the effusion of your blood? Please it you from henceforth to enterteine & keepe your good renoume, and defend your people, that without you may not long defend them against your enemies, to the ende, that wee may come to the victorie by your prowesse, by the which we hope to atteine and come to it.[1]
> [Rec.II.630; AH, 544]

Achilles, in a pessimistic frame of mind, thinks Helen not worth the cost in bloodshed [Rec.II.631; AH, 544]. So many nobles have been lost in combat that only "villaines" remain to people and govern the earth.

> And therfore in as much as ye require me to goe to battell, so much paine and labour loose yee, for I haue no more intention to put me any more in daunger: and loue better to loose my renowme then my life: for in the end there is no prowesse, but it will be forgotten. [Rec.II.631; AH, 544-45]

The Greek councilors return to report to Agamemnon their failure. The general assembly considers the possibility of peace, but not for long, since Calchas in no uncertain terms reminds them of the victory foretold by the Gods [Rec.II.631; AH, 545-46].

The second visit Agamemnon and Nestor pay Achilles is more successful. To stem the Trojan advances, Achilles loans his Myrmidons, though he still refuses to fight.

> . . . and Agamemnon prayed him that would come forth to the battell, and suffer no more their people thus to be slaine,

---

1. For Lydgate's account, see Appendix I, ii.

> But Achilles woulde neuer stirre vp his courage for his
> words: yet forasmuch as he loued Agamemnon, he agreed
> and consented y^t his men should go to battell without him . . . .
>   [Rec.II.634; AH, 547; Troy Book, IV, 1681–1896]

HOMER

The incident of the Greek embassy to Achilles in the ninth book
of the Iliades is comparable to Shakespeare's in Act III, scene iii,
of Troilus and Cressida, though the method of treatment and the
content of thought are very dissimilar. During a particularly heavy
engagement in which the Greeks are being hard-pressed by the
Trojans Nestor advises the despondent Agamemnon to attempt to
win back Achilles' favor "by kind words and pleasing gifts."

> Euen now yet let vs seeke redresse; we see that
>   needs we must
> Confesse to Ioue, and to our friend, fitt compensation
>   yield,
> Whome fayre sweete speech and royall gifts, must
>   supple for the field.   [Iliades, p. 79]

Agamemnon, quick to give offense, is not slow to ask for forgive-
ness. He perceives that though he is king, he is really king of only
numbers and general weaknesses.

> Myne owne offence, myne owne tongue graunts, one
>   man must stad in fight
> For our whole armie; him I wrongde, him Ioue loues
>   from his hart:
> He shewes it in thus honoring him, who liuing thus
>   apart
> Proues vs but number: for his want, makes all our
>   weaknes seene:
> Yet after my confest offence, soothing my humorous
>   spleene,
> Ile sweeten his affects againe, with presents
>   infinite . . . .   [p. 79]

Nestor recommends Phoenix, Ajax, and prince Ulysses as legates
most fit to undertake the mission. Ulysses, the first to appeal to
Achilles, does not minimize the helplessness of the Greek host without his aid. He directly urges him to return to combat.

> And I am seriously afraide, heauen will performe his
>   [Hector's] threates
> And that t'is fatall to vs all, far from our natiue
>   seates
> To perish in victorious Troy, but rise though it be
>   late.
> Deliuer the afflicted Greekes, from Troys tumultuous
>   hate;
> It will hereafter be thy griefe, when no strength
>   can suffice:

> To remedy th'effected threates, of our calamities;
> Consider these affaires in time, while thou maist
>   vse thy power.   [pp. 82-83]

Ulysses recalls to Achilles the advice his father Peleus gave him
before he left for the war.

> My sonne (said he) the victorie, let Ioue and Pallas
>   vse
> At their high pleasures, but do thou, no honorde
>   meanes refuse:
> That may aduance her; in fit boundes, contayne thy
>   mightie minde,
> Nor let the knowledge of thy strength, be factiously
>   enclinde
> Contriuing mischiefes; be to fame and generall good
>   profest
> The more will all sortes honor thee, benignity is
>   best.
> Thus chargde thy Syre, which thou forgetst . . . .   [p. 83]

To appease Achilles, Ulysses enumerates in great detail the many
and costly gifts that Agamemnon offers as a token of appeasement.
For Achilles, however, no present gift can cancel past injuries.

> Nor Atreus sonne, nor al the Greekes shall winne
>   me to their aide:
> Their sute is wretchedlie enforst to free their owne
>   despaires:
> And my life neuer shal be hyrde with thankeles
>   desperate prayers.   [p. 84]

The treasures that Agamemnon offers are no compensation for
the loss of his life which Fate will bring about if he remains in Troy
[p. 87]. Phoenix, by an historical parable, warns Achilles that if he
refuses to aid the Greeks until their plight becomes extreme, he will
have the fighting without the compensation that Agamemnon is now
in a position to give him. Achilles remains as obdurate to the old
man's suit as he is to that of Ajax.

> But still as often as I thinke, how rudely I was
>   vsde,
> And like a stranger for all rites, fit for our
>   good refusde;
> My hart doth swell against the man, that durst be
>   so prophane
> To violate his sacred place: not for my priuate bane,
> But since wrackt vertues generall laws, he shameles
>   did infrindge,
> For whose sake I will lose the raynes, and giue
>   mine anger swindge,
> Without my wisdomes least impeach . . . .   [p. 94]

At the end of the embassy, Achilles is as firm in his position as
at the beginning. His pride, as Diomedes points out, has only been
increased by the legates' words [p. 95].

HEYWOOD

The first embassy to Achilles, as Heywood dramatized the incident in the Iron Age, is not a formal embassy. No special legates
are sent by either Agamemnon or Nestor to remind Achilles of his
responsibilities. During a heavy engagement in which the Trojan
"champaigne" "Is made a standing poole of Greekish blood," Achilles
idles away the time playing the lute [Dr. Wks. III.311].[2] As the Greek
leaders, singly and in succession, on their way from the field pass
by Achilles, they stop to urge him to return to combat. Achilles ignores Ajax, the first to summon him. When Agamemnon asks, "Can
our great Champion touch a womanish Lute, And heare the grones
of twenty thousand soules Gasping their last breath," Achilles replies,
"I can" [III. 311]. Menelaus draws no response of consequence
from the haughty Myrmidon leader. Ajax and Ulysses together, however, are able to prevail on him to lend them his troops, which Patroclus appears eager to lead.
    When Hector is slain, Achilles returns to the seclusion of his tent
once more, to keep his vow to Hecuba to kill no more Trojans, even
though he has broken it by slaying her first-born, Hector. Nonethe-
less he withdraws a second time. Ulysses, who is second ambassa-
dor and apparently acts without orders from Agamemnon, has no
difficulty in making clear to Achilles that if he slays the second Hector, Troilus, he will be able to pass unhindered through the gates
of Troy and make Polyxena his own. If, on the other hand, Troilus
succeeds in slaying all the Greeks and wrings terms of peace from
them, it will not then be so easy for Achilles to become Priam's
son [III. 325]. Achilles' response is immediate:

> My sword and armour,
> Arise my bleeding ministers of death,
> I'le feast you with an Ocean of blood-royall:
> Vlysses, ere this Sunne fall from the skies,
> By this right hand the warlike Troilus dyes. [III. 325]

    In studying the composition of separate incidents in Troilus and
Cressida, it has been possible to note with fair certainty what episodes from the different versions of the siege of Troy Shakespeare
selected for his play, what changes he made, and frequently why he
altered his original source. His treatment of the embassy to Achilles,
on the other hand, has so few elements that are common to the other
versions, that one cannot be certain to which account he was indebted.
He could have selected the incident of the embassy from either Homer,
or Lydgate, or Caxton (or from Heywood if the Iron Age was in existence then), but in any case he could not handle the scene as his predecessors had done because he had radically altered the original
purpose of the embassy for dramatic reasons. That in turn
demanded a change in content.

2. Cf. Iliades, p. 81. Achilles' harp has become a lute in Heywood.

The purpose of the embassy in all the earlier accounts under consideration is clear and straightforward. It is to beg or persuade Achilles to return to combat. In Troilus and Cressida, though the return of Achilles is the ultimate purpose of the embassy, the more immediate reason for it is to illustrate the working of Ulysses' policy, the stratagem by which he expects to goad Achilles to action. During the first embassy—and it is necessary to note Ajax among the legates—the Greek leaders, following Ulysses' plan, play up the virtues of Ajax. Before Achilles' tent, he is proclaimed the better man. In the second embassy, Ulysses sees Achilles alone. He attempts to stir up his passion by showing to him the position in the host Ajax now holds, a position he owes of course to Ulysses' machinations. Though he makes clear to Achilles that Ajax is no "great and complete man," Ulysses notes that he has "communicated his parts to others," and already the Grecian lords

> . . . clap the lubber Ajax on the shoulder
> As if his foot were on brave Hector's breast
> And great Troy shrieking.   [III.iii.139–41]

While Achilles rests on the merits of good deeds past, which are soon forgotten when many press one another for glory in war, Ajax has caught the eye of the host and has the reputation Achilles once possessed.

In other versions considered, the embassy is a suit; in Troilus and Cressida, it is part of a plot. It is the dramatic illustration of Ulysses' stratagem whose purpose is to stir Achilles from his lethargy by showing him what he has lost, and what sort of man now has what he has lost. It will be enough, Ulysses suspects, to rouse this "great and complete man" to action. It is obvious, therefore, that Shakespeare could not follow his authors without dropping the stratagem that was foreshadowed in Act I, scene iii. For the staff to take gifts to Achilles or to entreat him to return would only increase his already overweening pride, and would entirely defeat the purpose of the stratagem. Furthermore, insinuation that another is possibly better than he, the voicing of regret that he no longer holds the position he deserves, is better psychology to use in handling the pride of an Achilles.

Shakespeare worked the original episode into his plan. He skillfully fitted it into the challenge plot. It will be recalled that in Section 4, above, the observation was made that the incident of the challenge which is in Homer a mere episode without duration, without dramatic build-up, and without relation to Achilles' position, Shakespeare developed into the dramatic situation of the war plot. The dramatic purpose of the challenge was to be a lever to force Achilles to take action by arousing his jealousy of Ajax's prowess. To accomplish this task, Ulysses first "arranged" the lottery so that Ajax would be selected to meet Hector. Secondly, he devised his stratagem, which was to raise Ajax to the highest position in the host: so high, in fact, that Achilles to regain his lost renown

would be forced to fight for it. And the embassy scenes, which are
the representation of this policy, Shakespeare reinterpreted in
order to give them a direct bearing on the larger situation of the
challenge.

Since Shakespeare so altered the original episode of the embassy
to fit his purpose, no affinity with earlier accounts is to be expected. It might be noticed, however, that in the Iliades [p. 80] Ajax is
one of the legates chosen. In the Iron Age Ajax is the first to beg
Achilles for aid [Dr.Wks. III.310]. But the situation Shakespeare
developed demanded the presence of Ajax.

Seemingly the dramatist owed little to the words Achilles and
Ulysses exchange in the sources. Lydgate's Ulysses tells Achilles
he is stubborn not to take advantage of Fortune who has all along
favored him, and still would increase his fame if he but exerted
himself.

> . . . youre highe renoun
> Atteyned hath the exaltacioun
> And highest prikke of Fortunys whele,
> It were gret wronge, and ye loke wele,
> Of wilfulnes for to be vnkynde
> To hir that ye so frendly to you fynde,
>
> . . . .
> Wherfore, allas, whi wil ye suffer passe
> Youre noble fame, of verray wilfulnes,
> While it is hiest in his worthiness?
> [Troy Book, IV. 1749 ff.]

Achilles replies that Fame is not permanent: Fame is a wind
that blows for a short time.

> For worthines, after deth I-blowe,
> Is but a wynde, & lasteth but a throwe;
> For though renoun & pris be blowe wyde,
> Foryetilnes leith it ofte a-syde
> By lengthe of yeris and obliuioun,
> Thorugh envie and fals collucioun.[3]   [IV. 1871 ff.]

The conversation in Caxton is more terse. Ulysses urges Achilles
to return to battle in order to keep his name bright. "Please it you
from henceforth to enterteine & keepe your good renoume." But Achilles replies that all deeds of greatness are soon forgotten. ". . . I
haue no more intention to put me any more in daunger: and loue
better to loose my renowme then my life: for in the end there is
no prowesse, but it be forgotten" [Rec.II.631; AH, 545].

Homer's Achilles, however, rejects proposals to return to the
fight, because, he notes, worth is not truly honored. The hero and
coward get like deserts.

___

3. W. B. Drayton Henderson (Essays, pp. 148-49) suggests Shakespeare used this passage.

Eauen share hath he that keepes his tent, and he to
    field doth goe.
With equall honor Cowardes dye, and men most valiant.
The much performer and the man, that can of nothing
    vant.
No ouerplus I euer found, when with my mindes most
    strife,
To do them good to dangerous fight, I haue exposde
    my life.   [Iliades, p. 84]

6. The Combat

SHAKESPEARE

Hector's challenge, which Aeneas presents to the assembled Greeks
in Act I, scene iii, does not come to an issue until Act IV, scene v.
After Ajax has his trumpet sounded to summon Hector from Troy,
and after Cressida, on her way to her father's tent, has exchanged
pleasantries with the Greek leaders, Aeneas and the Trojan chiefs,
in answer to the trumpet, enter the Grecian camp. Aeneas, in Hector's name, asks what kind of battle the Greeks intend.

Hail, all ye state of Greece! what shall be done
To him that victory commands? or do you purpose
A victor shall be known? will you the knights
Shall to the edge of all extremity
Pursue each other, or shall they be divided
By any voice or order of the field?   [IV. v. 65 – 70]

Agamemnon asks that Hector prescribe the terms of combat,
since he is the challenger. Aeneas explains the difficulty of Hector's position.

This Ajax is half made of Hector's blood:
In love whereof half Hector stays at home;
Half heart, half hand, half Hector comes to seek
This blended knight, half Trojan, and half Greek.
                              [I V. v. 83 – 86]

Agamemnon appoints Diomedes as representative to stand by Ajax
to determine with Aeneas the length and nature of the contest.

Here is Sir Diomed. Go, gentle knight,
Stand by our Ajax: as you and Lord Aeneas
Consent upon the order of their fight,
So be it; either to the uttermost,
Or else a breath . . . .   [IV. v. 88 – 92]

After Ajax and Hector have exchanged blows that are fatal to
neither combatant, Diomedes proclaims an end, if it is agreeable
to the challenger.

```
Agam.      They are in action.
Nest.      Now, Ajax, hold thine own!
Tro.                    Hector, thou sleep'st;
Awake thee!
Agam.      His blows are well dispos'd:
there Ajax!
Dio.       You must no more.
           . . . . . . . . . . . . . . . . .
Ajax.      I am not warm yet; let us
fight again.
Dio.       As Hector pleases.        [IV. v. 113-19]
```

It pleases Hector to undertake no further action. He has no appe-
tite for a battle against one who is his own kin.

                    Why, then I will no more:
Thou art, great lord [Ajax], my father's sister's son,
A cousin-german to great Priam's seed;
The obligation of our blood forbids
A gory emulation 'twixt us twain.
Were thy commixion Greek and Trojan so
That thou could'st say, "This hand is Grecian all,
And this is Trojan; the sinews of this leg
All Greek, and this all Troy; my mother's blood
Runs on the dexter cheek, and this sinister
Bounds in my father's"; by Jove multipotent,
Thou should'st not bear from me a Greekish member
Wherein my sword had not impressure made
Of our rank feud: but the just gods gainsay
That any drop thou borrow'dst from thy mother,
My sacred aunt, should by my mortal sword
Be drain'd!   [IV. v. 119-38]

Thus Hector's answer to the "expectance here from both the sides/
What further you will do" is embracement [IV. v. 146-48].

CAXTON

In the Recuyell, the fight between Ajax and Hector takes place at
an early period during the siege of Troy. It is an incident in the
second battle between the two opposed forces that occurs on the day
after the Greeks successfully attained a foothold on the Trojan plain,
but before they had consolidated their position [Rec.II.575; AH, 496].
Among the many Greek and Trojan leaders who fought single combats that day were Ajax and Hector. Their meeting was accidental.
Hector, seeking in the general press those warriors who were inflicting the greatest harm on his own forces, found in one of these
powerful combatants his cousin, Ajax. The brief combat they engage
in, which is broken off at Ajax's request, is an incidental fight in
the day's melee. It is not a formal combat. No challenge had pre-
ceded it.

In this day had ye Troyans had victory of the Greeks, if
fortune had consented: for they might haue slaine thē al,
and eschewed great euils that after came to thē. Certes it
is not wisedome, when any man findeth his ennemy in great
perill and fortune, to offer his power to deliuer him thereof:
for it happened oftentimes, that he shall neuer recouer to
haue his enemy in the same case, but that fortune will turne
her backe: Thus it happeneth this day to the vnhappie Hector,
that had the better of his ennemies, and might haue slaine
them all, if he hadde would, for they sought nothing but for
to flea. When by great misaduenture there came afore him
in an encounter Thelamon Aiax that was sonne of king Thelamon, and Exion, that was coosin Germaine of Hector and of
his brethren, which was wise and valiant, he addressed him
against Hector, and deliuered to him a great assault, and
Hector to him, as they that were valiannt both two: and as
they were fighting, they spake and talked togither, and thereby Hector knew that he was cosin Germaine, sonne of his
aunt: and then Hector for courtesse embraced him in his
armes, and made great cheere, and offered to him to doe all
his pleasure, if hee desired any thing of him, and praied him
that he would come to Troy with him, for to see his linage
of his mothers side: but the said Thelamon, that intended to
nothing but to his aduauntage, saide that he would not go at
this time. But praied Hector, requesting that if he loued him
so much as he said, he would for his sake, and at his instance,
ceasse the battaile for that day, and that the Troyans shoulde
leaue the Greekes in peace. The vnhappy Hector accorded to
him his request, and blewe a horne, and made all his people
to withdraw into the Citie. Then hadde the Troyans begunne
to put the fire in the shippes of the Greekes, and had all burnt
them, had not Hector called them from thence . . .
      This was the cause wherefore the Troyans missed to haue
the victorie, to the which they might neuer after attaine, nor
come: for fortune was to them contrary. . . .

[Rec.II.589-90; AH, 507-8]

In the Recuyell, the outcome of the meeting between Ajax and Hector is of vital consequence to the history of the war. Though the contest takes place at an early date, it is the turning point of the war,
since the Trojans from then on never regain the positions they held
when Hector summoned them to retreat.

HOMER

Hector's challenge is an incident in Book VII of the Iliades. It is
proposed by "The God that beares the siluer Bowe and warrs tri-
umphant maide," as those deities view the battlefield from "Ioues
broad beech," in order to stop the general carnage that results from
the conflicts between the Greek and Trojan forces.

> . . . we will direct the spirit, that burnes in
>   Hectors brest,
> To challenge any Greeke to wounds, with single
>   powers imprest:
> Which Greekes admiring will accept, and make some
>   one stand out,
> T'encounter so diuine a foe, with a conceipt as
>   stout.   [Iliades, p. 47]

There is no appreciable lapse of time between Hector's deliver-
ance of the challenge and its issue in combat. As soon as lots are
cast [p. 51], and Ajax is selected [p. 51] and armed [p. 52], the opponents take the field. Ajax, whose appearance "shooke the ioynts,
Of all the Troianes," and even made Hector tremble and momen-
tarily regret the challenge [p. 52], opened the fight.

> Now Hector thou shalt clearlie know, thus meeting
>   man to man,
> What other leaders arme our host, besides great
>   Thetis sonne:[1]
> Who with his hardie Lions hart, hath armies ouerrunne.
> But he lies at our crookt-sternde fleete a riual with
>   our king
> In height of spirite, yet to Troy he manie kings did
>   bring,
> Coequall with EAacides, al able to sustaine,
> All thy bould chalenge can import: begin then, wordes
>   are vain.   [p. 52]

Hector's reply, before he hurls his javelin, is that of one confi-
dent in his skill of arms.

> Prince of the Souldiers came from Greece, assay
>   not me like one,
> Yong and immartiall, with puft ayre, or like an
>   amazon dame
> I haue the habit of all fights and know the bloodie
>   frame:
> Of manlie slaughter: I well know the readie right
>   hand charge:
> I know the left, and euerie sway of my securefull
>   targe;
> I triumph in the crueltie, of fixed combat fight,
> Manage my horse to all designes, I thinke then with
>   good right,
> I may be confident as farre, as this my challenge
>   goes.   [pp. 52-53]

The combat itself is described in considerable detail [p. 53]. Hector, though he is evenly matched with Ajax, receives more serious
blows than he is able to give.

---

1. Shakespeare's Ajax thinks he is as good a man as Achilles.—Troilus and Cressida, II.iii.151–67.

> But Aiax a farre greater stone lift vp, and wreathing
>   round:
> With all his bodie layd to it, he sent it forth to
>   wound;
> And gaue vnmeasured force to it; the round stone broke
>   within
> His rundled target: his strong knees to languish did
>   begin:
> He streaking leand vpon his shield, but Phoebus
>   raisd him straight.　　　　　　　　　　[p. 53]

As the fighting is resumed, and passes to close combat, the heralds, the "messingers of gods and godlike men," interpose their sceptres between Ajax and Hector, and stop the contest.

> . . . now no more my sonnes, the soueraigne of the
>   skyes
> Doth loue you both; both souldiers are, all witnesse
>   with good right:
> But now Night laies her mace on earth; t'is good
>   t'obay the night.　　　　　　　　　　[p. 54]

Ajax, conforming to the code of knighthood, refers the decision of the combat to the challenger. Hector, not averse to postponing the fight until that day when Jove will be the herald, relinquishes his arms.[2]

> Ajax, since Ioue to thy bigge forme, made thee so
>   strong a man,
> And gaue thee skill to vse they [sic] strength; so much
>   that for thy speare,
> Thou art most excellent of Greece, now let vs fight
>   forbeare:
> Hereafter we shall warre again, till Ioue our Herald
>   be,
> And grace with conquest, which he will; heauen yields
>   to night, and wee.　　　　　　　　　　[p. 54]

HEYWOOD

In the Iron Age, Hector sends a challenge to that Greek who believes he has valor enough to meet him in single combat [Dr.Wks. III.296]. There is no lapse of time between the delivery of the challenge and the fight. It is fought between Ajax and Hector as soon as the lots are drawn and the opponents are made ready. Hector, at once, has qualms about fighting his own blood.

> And Cuz, by Ioue thou hast a braue aspect,
> It cheeres my blood to looke on such a foe:

2. Cf. the formal procedure of the combat as it occurs in the 1598 edition of the epic with Shakespeare's portrayal, Troilus and Cressida, IV. v. 64 ff.

I would there ran none of our Troian blood
In all thy veines, or that it were diuided
From that which thou receiuest from Telamon:
Were I assured our blood possest one side,
And that the other; by Olimpicke Ioue,
I'd thrill my Iauelin at the Grecian moysture,
And spare the Troian blood: Aiax I loue it
Too deare to shed it, I could rather wish
Achilles the halfe god of your huge army,
Had beene my opposite.   [Dr. Wks.III.299]

Though Achilles remains out of the combat, Ajax is quick to remind Hector that he is not second in mind or in strength to Achilles.

Hee keepes his Tent
In mournful passion that he mist the combate:
But Hector, I shall giue thee cause to say,
There's in the Greekish hoast a Knight a Prince,
As Lyon hearted, and as Gyant strong
As Thetis sonne: behold my warlicke Target . . . . [III. 299]

There is a brief description of the battle in a stage direction
which is in part a condensation of Homer's account:

Alarum, in this combate both hauing lost their swords and
Shields. Hector takes vp a great peece of a Rocke, and casts
at Aiax; who tears a young Tree vp by the rootes, and
assailes Hector, at which they are parted by both armes.
                                                    [III. 300]

Agamemnon stops the contest, lest too much blood be shed. Hector,
as challenger, gives the word of cessation so that each combatant
will have terms of equal honor [Ibid.]. Hector extends a "cousins
hand" [Ibid.] and, after an exchange of gifts, the armies disperse.

A combat between Ajax and Hector is an incident in the Iliades,
Troy Book,[3] the Recuyell, Troilus and Cressida, and the Iron Age.
In the version of the siege of Troy that Caxton translated, the fight
is a major event in the opening phase of the war that takes place
after the Greeks have attained a substantial foothold on the Trojan
coast but before they have been able to strengthen and adequately
defend their positions. During a general melee, Hector ranging
through the hosts in search of the enemy, who is cutting most de-
cisively into the Trojan ranks, singles out a substantial opponent,
and crosses swords with him. Before the battle becomes fatal, Hector, recognizing in his opponent a kinsman, breaks off the combat.
Hector cannot shed his own blood.
    The battle is, according to both Caxton and Lydgate, of vital con-
sequence to the Trojans. Because he is his kinsman, Hector grants
Ajax his request that for the remainder of the day the Trojan forces

3. Troy Book, III, 2036–2148. For pertinent excerpts, see Appendix I, ii.

will withdraw from their advanced positions and no more engage in
fight. Hector withdraws his troops and by so doing, since they were
about to fire the Greek ships and despoil the enemy in his encamp-
ment, loses for Troy the early advantage it had won for achieving
victory.

In the mediaeval narrative, the combat is an important incident.
Though it takes place at an early stage of the campaign, and though
it was casual and not the result of a challenge, the outcome marks
the turning point of the war —and all because of consanguinity.

The combat in the Iliades is fought in the last and ninth year
of the war. The meeting between Ajax and Hector is not casual.
Athene and Apollo, to arrest the general slaughter the combined
forces are inflicting on one another, propose a single combat, and
inspire Hector to send a challenge to any Greek who feels he can
match with him in skill in arms. To determine the opponent, Nestor proposes a lottery. Ajax wins it, and after he is sufficiently
prepared for battle, enters the field against Hector.

Though the gods had decreed the fight would not be mortal [p. 47],
it is sharp and Hector proves himself not quite the match for Ajax
he had expected to be. Only by the intervention of Apollo is he saved
from severe injury [p. 53].

The battle is interrupted by the heralds, and broken off by Hector, for no other reason than that it is night [p. 54]. The battle itself
has no consequence. It marks no special phase of the war. It is
merely a duel, which stops short of fatality.

Shakespeare treated the combat differently from any of his predecessors, though the incident itself is a composition of elements derived from his sources. There can be no doubt that Shakespeare
selected the episode from the Iliades, since it is the only extant
version that definitely precedes Troilus and Cressida in which the
combat is linked with the challenge. The situation is the same in
both accounts, with the exception that the challenge in the Iliades
is immediately followed by the combat, whereas in Troilus and
Cressida there is a lapse of time. The necessity for Shakespeare's
altering the time sequence was discussed in Section 4, above. Furthermore, in both accounts Ajax is selected by lottery, though U-
lysses in the drama arranges that Ajax be selected for reasons
explained above in Section 4. And, lastly, the combat occurs in the
last years of the siege.

The reasons for disjoining battle, however, are different. In the
Iliades, Hector, on the herald's advice, breaks off combat because
it is night [p. 54]. In the play, Hector will not fight beyond the bounds
of what constitutes a "maiden battle" because Ajax is his kin. He
refuses to spill his own blood, though it is in another. Shakespeare
more probably lifted the un-Homeric motive from Caxton than from
Lydgate, and joined it to the episode he took from the Iliades.

If Shakespeare in selecting his material was looking for a treatment of the situation that was inherently dramatic, it is obvious
why he found the Caxton version more satisfactory to his purpose

than the Homeric. For one thing, a combat between kin sharpens
the interest in the conflict, and there were, for the Elizabethans,
more emotional and moral overtones involved in such an issue than
in a combat between strangers. Furthermore, to break off combat
because kin does not wish to slay kin is a reason more effective
than the mere fading of daylight. And lastly, Shakespeare, by adapting Caxton's account, thereby terminated the incident in a way that
did not make the whole incident and its action appear inconsequential.[4]

Heywood's handling of the combat in the Iron Age is so similar
to Shakespeare's that there can be no doubt that one dramatist
borrowed from the other. Though Heywood follows Homer more
closely in detail than does Shakespeare, his version combines the
Homeric episode with the Caxton motive for discontinuing the fight.
Furthermore, the speech in which Hector breaks off the fight is
similar to Hector's speech in Troilus and Cressida.[5] Since there is
no historical evidence that the Iron Age antedates Troilus and Cressida, Heywood may be regarded as the borrower.

7. Hector's Visit to the Greek Camp

SHAKESPEARE

In the last scene of the fourth act of Troilus and Cressida,
Hector, after he has ended the combat with his Greek cousin
on friendly terms, is invited by Ajax to stay to see the Grecian
camp.

> If I might in entreaties find success,
> As seld I have the chance, I would desire
> My famous cousin to our Grecian tents.
> [IV. v. 149–51]

Diomedes, who has acted as herald opposite to Aeneas during the
fight [IV. v. 88 ff], requests Hector, in Agamemnon's name, to stay.

> 'Tis Agamemnon's wish, and great Achilles
> Doth long to see unarm'd the valiant Hector.
> [IV. v. 152–53]

Hector accepts, and is welcomed by each of the Greek leaders
in turn. Agamemnon, though he "would be rid of such an enemy,"
for the "extant moment" welcomes great Hector "From heart of
very heart" [IV. v. 164, 168, 171]. Nestor extols his mercy and his

4. It should be observed that in the Iliades the "gods gainsay" a
mortal conflict on personal grounds (Iliades, p. 54), in Troilus and
Cressida on moral grounds. Shakespeare disengaged the Homeric
deities from direct participation in the action: they remain in the
background as guardians of moral behaviour.
5. See Tatlock, PMLA, XXX (1915), 751.

power, and mentions the time he knew his grandsire when he "once fought with him" [IV. v. 197]. Hector, meeting Ulysses, recalls the visit the latter made with Diomedes to Ilion on their embassy in the early stages of the war [IV. v. 215 ff.]. Achilles alone does not show the courtesy to Hector that marks the welcome of the other Greek leaders. He views Hector as his chief opponent, even though he is a guest.

> Now, Hector, I have fed mine eyes on thee;
> I have with exact view perus'd thee, Hector,
> And quoted joint by joint.   [IV. v. 231-33]

Hector glances briefly at Achilles, who chides him for the brevity of his glance. Achilles views Hector a second time "As I would buy thee, view thee limb by limb" [IV. v. 238].

> Tell me, you heavens, in which part of his body
> Shall I destroy him? whether there, or there,
>   or there?
> That I may give the local wound a name,
> And make distinct the very breath whereout
> Hector's great spirit flew. Answer me, heavens!
>   [IV. v. 242-46]

The sight of Hector unarmed, in his "weeds of peace," has roused Achilles' blood-lust. He lays his hand on Hector's as a wager to return to battle on the morrow.

> To-morrow do I meet thee, fell as death;
> To-night all friends.   [IV. v. 269-70]

CAXTON

The visit of Hector to the Greek camp in Troilus and Cressida is analogous to a situation in the Recuyell, though the details and the general treatment of the situation vary greatly in the two versions.

In the Recuyell, there is no combat that takes Hector to the Grecian camp. He is not specifically invited by any of the enemy leaders. During a truce in the siege, he "went on a day vnto the tentes of the Greekes" [Rec.II.602; AH, 519].[1] Achilles, who is one of the first to welcome him, is eager to see him unarmed and invites him to his tent.

> . . . and Achilles behelde him gladly, forasmuch as hee had neuer seen him vnarmed. And at the request of Achilles, Hector went into his Tent, and as they spake togither of many thinges, Achilles saide to Hector, I haue great pleasure to see thee vnarmed, forasmuch as I haue neuer seen thee before. But yet I shal haue more pleasure, when the day shall come that thou shalt die of my hand, which thing I most desire.   [Rec.II.602; AH, 519]

---

1. AH, 519; Troy Book, III.3762 ff. Pertinent passages are quoted in Appendix I, iv.

Caxton's Achilles has felt the strength of Hector in previous combats and has lost much blood at his hands. His anger for past injuries is great, his sorrow for the death of Patroclus still greater.

> For I knowe thee to be very strong, and I haue oftentimes prooued it, vnto the effusion of my bloud, whereof I haue great anger: and yet haue much more great sorrow, foras-much as thou slewest Patroclus, him that I most loued of the worlde. Then thou maiest beleeue for certain, that be-fore this yeare bee past, his death shalbe auenged vppon thee, by my hand, and also I wote well, that thou desirest to slea mee.   [Rec.II.602; AH, 519]

Hector is quick to assure Achilles that he will give him his due of death, if he is able, since he has come into Troy to lay waste its land and to destroy the peace.

> . . . if I desire thy death, maruell thou nothing thereof: for-asmuch as thou deseruest to bee mine ennemie mortall; thou art come unto our land for to destroie mee and mine. I will that thou knowe, that thy wordes feare mee nothing at all, but yet I haue hope that within two yeare, if I liue, and con-tinue in health, and my sworde faile mee not, thou shalt die by the force and valor of mine handes, not thou alonely, but all the most greatest of the Greeks.[Rec.II.602; AH, 519-20]

Hector then proposes that the issue of the war be settled by a personal combat between them. Achilles agrees to the suggestion.

> And if thou [Achilles] thinke that thou bee so strong, that thou maiest defend thee against mee, make it so that all the barons of thine hoste promise and accord that wee fight body against body, and if it happen that thou vanquish me, that my friendes and I shalbe banished out of this realme, and we shall leaue it vnto the Greekes, and thereof I shall leaue good pledge. And heerin thou maiest profite to many other, that may run in great danger, if they haunt the battaile: and if it happen that I vanquishe thee, make that all they of thy hoste depart hence, and suffer vs to liue in peace. Achilles . . . gaue to Hector his gage, which Hector tooke . . . .
> [Rec.II.603; AH, 520]

Agamemnon, who has heard of the bargain Hector and Achilles have made between them, and is perhaps not too sure of the in-vincibility of the Myrmidon Chief, hastens to Achilles and quashes the idea of a personal conflict to decide so grave an issue.[Rec.II. 603; AH, 520].

HOMER

There is no situation in the Iliades comparable to that in Troilus and Cressida in which Hector visits the Grecian camp. Conversation between enemy warriors is exchanged on the battle-field rather than in the camp. In Book XXII of the Iliad, however, there is a brief

passage which is suggestive of Achilles' words to Hector in the play.
Towards the close of the epic, after Hector has been driven about
the Trojan walls by the fast following Achilles, and after Hector
has decided to take his stand and fight his opponent, Achilles, as his
enemy stands before him, appraises Hector's body to determine the
most vulnerable spot.

> His bright and sparkling eyes
> Look'd through the body of his foe, and sought through
>   all that prise
> The next way to his thirsted life. Of all ways, only one
> Appear'd to him, and that was where th'unequal winding
>   bone,
> That joins the shoulders and the neck, had place, and
>   where there lay
> The speeding way to death; and there his quick eyes
>   could display
> The place it sought, e'en through those arms his friend
>   Patroclus wore
> When Hector slew him. There he aim'd and there his
>   jav'lin tore
> Stern passage quite through Hector's neck; yet miss'd
>   it so his throat
> It gave him pow'r to change some words.[2]

HEYWOOD

There are a great many incidents in the five acts of the first part
of the Iron Age, and one that receives much elaboration of treatment
is the association of Greeks and Trojans immediately following the
combat [Dr.Wks. III. 300–9]. However, the inviter here is Hector,
and all the Greeks journey to Troy where the entertainment is sumptu-
ous, and Helen appears as the star of the feast. It is on this occasion
(Patroclus has long since been dead), that Achilles, seeing Priam's
daughter Polyxena at table, is suddenly overcome by love.

> Hec. Priam vnto the Greekish General
> This profer makes. Because these blood-stayn'd
>   fields
> Are ouer-spread with slaughter, to take truce
> Till all the dead on both sides be interr'd:
> Which if you grant, he here inuites the Generall,
> His nephew Aiax, and the great Achilles,
> With twenty of your chiefe selected Princes,
> To banquet with him in his royal Pallace:
> Those reuels ended, then to armes againe . . . [III.300–1]

Attending the party and dance are the Greek leaders, Agamemnon,
Menelaus, Ulysses, and the warriors Achilles, Ajax, and Diomedes..

---

2. The Iliads of Homer, ed. Richard Hooper (London, 1857), II.
xxii.275 ff.

Also among the guests are Calchas and Cressida. Though the banquet
on one occasion almost breaks up [Dr.Wks. 304–5], at no time, quite
naturally, does the exchange between Hector and Achilles take place.
But Achilles, as he sees Hector, notes that

> this Troian Hector
> Out-shines Achilles and his polisht honours
> Ecclipseth our bright glory, till hee set
> Wee cannot rise.   [III. 303]

A comparative analysis of the episode in which Hector visits the
Greek camp reveals that Shakespeare departed from his authors in
adapting the incident for stage presentation. He left out material
from the earlier versions and made some additions. He expanded
parts of the conversation between Achilles and Hector into dramatic
dialogue, and above all, by altering the original position of the visit,
he fitted it into the sequence of dramatic action, and thereby supplied
a logical reason for a rather extraordinary visit where one did not
formerly exist.

The episode itself does not occur in the Iliades. In the Iron Age
it is not the same situation, nor is the place of meeting the same.
But both Lydgate and Caxton describe the meeting.

Dramatically, the scene serves more than one purpose, and in
Shakespeare's adaptation of it from Caxton, more probably than
from Lydgate, one can see evidence of his stagecraft. In the first
place, the sight of Hector in his "weeds of peace" arouses Achilles
from lethargy and kindles in him a desire to see the "maiden
battle" he has recently witnessed turn into a mortal combat. Only
he will replace Ajax, and show Greeks and Trojans alike what an
Achilles is in combat.

> To-morrow do I meet thee fell as death;
> To-night all friends.

Ulysses' stratagem to arouse Achilles, and on the outcome of which
expectation has so long hung, seems to have fallen short of its purpose,
since Achilles witnessed the combat throughout and gave no indication
of an intention to withdraw from his isolation. But his silence throughout the combat is ominous, and effective; and the violence of his
attack on Hector when he greets him following the fight indicates the
change his mind was undergoing during the combat. Ulysses' policy
is vindicated; and Achilles is ready to return to the fight. Later
during the evening he exclaims to Patroclus:

> I'll heat his blood with Greekish wine to-night;
> Which with my scimiter I'll cool to-morrow.

In the second place, the disintegration that has so long postponed
activity seems now at an end; and the audience is prepared for the
denouement with the fall of Hector. In this final scene of the fourth
act is the "recuyell" of the forces for the final struggle made
certain by Achilles' pledge of hands with Hector to meet him on the
morrow.

If such are the principal reasons that prompted Shakespeare to
select this particular episode from the many in Caxton, how he
changed the episode is even more obvious. In the Recuyell, Hector
"went on a day vnto the tents of the Greekes." Shakespeare shifted
the episode to follow the combat, and by so doing, gave Hector a
logical reason for being in an unusual position. Also Shakespeare
omitted much of the conversation that takes place between the protagonists in the narrative. He did not transfer to the drama Achilles'
complaint of the many wounds he received from Hector; he has, of
course, since he was following the Homeric plan of major incidents,
no mention of Patroclus' death; he eschewed the moral discussion
as to the right of the Greek transgression on peaceful Trojan soil;
and he omitted all reference to Hector's proposal that he and Achilles,
by single combat, decide the issue of the war. Obviously such a plan
was as useless to Shakespeare as it was displeasing to Agamemnon.

But in Achilles' charge that "the day shall come that thou shalt
die of my hande" [Rec.II.602; AH, 519] is the definite suggestion for
the Shakespearean Achilles' charge that he will make a breach to
let out Hector's spirit. And Hector's boast to Achilles, Shakespeare
likewise developed from the Recuyell when Hector in reply promises
to slay his opponent in the battle that will come. "But yet I haue
hope that within two yeare if I liue, and my sworde faile mee not,
thou shalt die by the force and valor of mine handes, not thou alonely,
but all the most greatest of the Greeks" [Rec.II.602; AH, 519–20].
The charges and counter-charges of the protagonists of the play
have their origins in Caxton's narrative.

But a more striking resemblance between the two accounts is
confined to the desire Achilles has to see Hector unarmed. Caxton's
Achilles' "great pleasure to see thee vnarmed" [Rec II.602; AH, 519]
is strikingly close in words and in cadence to Shakespeare's "great
Achilles Doth long to see unarm'd the valiant Hector" [IV. v. 152–53].
But Shakespeare went one step farther than Caxton; he supplied a
reason for Achilles' desire.

The reason, namely to determine the part of Hector's body where
he will make the fatal breach, has an extraordinary similarity to
that expressed in the lines quoted from the Iliad. Though the situations are not analogous, the thoughts expressed are.

> His bright and sparkling eyes
> Look'd through the body of his foe, and sought
> through all that prise
> The next way to his thirsted life. Of all ways
> only one
> Appear'd to him.   [Iliads, xxii.275 ff.]

If Shakespeare had recourse to the Iliad for amplification of
the suggestion he got from Caxton, his "lesse Greeke" enabled him
to read the original, since Book XXII, in which the quoted passage
occurs, was not translated at the time he wrote the play. Except in
this instance, and in his treatment of Hector's death, Shakespeare

shows no specific indication in Troilus and Cressida that he went
outside the books Chapman translated for material.[3] Looking beneath
the surface of Caxton's description, and expanding his suggestions,
Shakespeare could have produced a resemblance to Homer's des-
scription without any direct knowledge of his text, and without un-
duly taxing our sense of the probability of the coincidence.

The meeting between Hector and the Greek leaders is Shakespeare's own contribution to the scene, although in the conversation
exchanged there are allusions to events which Caxton and Lydgate
had described in some detail. Nestor's reference to Hector's
"grandsire," with whom he once fought, is an incident in the first
destruction of Troy [Rec.II.349; AH, 289; Troy Book, II, 4084 ff.].
Hector recognizes Ulysses from the day when he and Diomedes under-
took their embassy to Ilion in an effort to regain Helen without re-
sorting to force of arms [Rec.II.558 ff.; AH, 482 ff.; Troy Book, II,
6720 ff.].

Interesting also is the possible relation of Robert Greene's contribution to the Trojan saga to Shakespeare's scene. In that conversation piece, Euphues his censure to Philautus (1587), the Greek
and Trojan warriors meet to discuss the true qualities of knighthood,
and each warrior tells a brief story to illustrate his conception of
the perfect knight. For our purpose, the first meeting of the leaders
is noteworthy.

> . . . they resolued vppon a truce for thirty dayes during which
> time, the Troian Ladies . . . namely Andromache, Cassandra,
> and Polixena, accompanied with Hector, Troilus, Aeneas,
> Helenus, and diuers other royall parentage, went to see the
> Gretian tents peopled with their enemies.[4] [Achilles' com-
> panions] weare Vlisses, Diomedes, Patroclus, with many
> Lordes of great, valour and progenie. The Gretians thus
> marching on in order met Hector who was first of his com-
> panie, whose very face harboring an extraordinary kinde of
> maiestie gaue them all to knowe, by supposition, that this
> was he which by his valour had made such dismal massacres,
> euen to their very Pauillions. Letting him and the rest of his
> crue passe with an enuious courtesie, as feeling in their mindes
> the scarres of his man-hoode: at last Achilles and hee came
> within view, who neuer hauing seene each other before, but
> in armor as enemies manacing reuenge in the field, stood a
> long time as men in a trance, till Hector burst forth into
> speaches.[5]
>   . . . Agamemnon accompanied with aged Nestor and other
> Lordes, stoode at the doore of Achilles tent redie to inter-
> tayne the Troians who with the rest dismounting from their

3. See below, Section 12 for his treatment of Hector's death.
4. The Life and Works of Robert Greene, ed. Alexander B. Grosart
(London, 1881–3), VI, 156.
5. Ibid., VI, 157.

horse. Hector pazing hand in hand with Achilles, Troilus with Vlisses.[6]

It is possible that Shakespeare was mindful of Greene's description of the meeting of the enemy leaders when he wrote the last scene of Act IV. In none of the primary sources is there so detailed an account of the grouping of characters. In the Iliades, when Ajax and Hector fight, most of the nobles from both sides are presumably there; in the Recuyell, Hector visits Achilles who has desired to see the Trojan unarmed, but no occasion is made of a visit with the Greek nobles. The formal meeting as it takes place in the play is not unlike that in Greene's account: and the leaders who comprise the gathering are the same, with the exception of Helenus, who does not appear in this scene in the play.

8. Hector and Andromache

SHAKESPEARE

Hector, usually amenable to admonishment [V. iii.1-2], cannot be deterred from entering combat on the fatal day, either by the entreaties of Andromache and Priam, or by the prophecies of Cassandra, because he has made a vow to the Gods to sally forth and fight for Troy. Andromache, who has dreamed

> Of bloody turbulence, and this whole night
> Hath nothing [seen] but shapes and forms
>   of slaughter,   [V. iii.11-12]

cannot dissuade Hector from performing his vow. Cassandra's observation that "The gods are deaf to hot and peevish vows" [V. iii.16] which to them are "more abhorr'd/Than spotted livers in the sacrifice" [V. iii.17-18] cannot move the man who finds more honor in keeping a pledge, though it is wrong, than in breaking it, though it is wise to do so.

Troilus, who is bent on seeking vengeance on Diomedes this day is disregardful of Andromache's wish, and is Hector's evil genius in this scene. He dismisses the "bodements" of Cassandra [V. iii. 78 ff.]; he disparages Hector's show of mercy and fair play in combat.

>   For the love of all the gods,
> Let's leave the hermit pity with our mothers,
> And when we have our armours buckled on,
> The venom'd vengeance ride upon our swords,
> Spur them to ruthful work, rein them from ruth.
>   [V.iii.44-48]

---

6. Ibid., VI, 164. As in Troilus and Cressida, V,ii, Ulysses and Troilus travel together in the Grecian camp.

Priam, summoned to lend his voice against Hector, supports the women's plea.

> Thy wife hath dream'd; thy mother hath had
>   visions;
> Cassandra doth foresee; and I myself
> Am like a prophet suddenly enrapt,
> To tell thee that this day is ominous:
> Therefore, come back.   [V.iii.63–67]

But Hector remains adamant.

> Aeneas is a-field;
> And I do stand engag'd to many Greeks,
> Even in the faith of valour, to appear
> This morning to them . . . .
> I must not break my faith.   [V.iii.67–71]

CAXTON

Caxton describes Hector's last day in Troy in greater detail than Shakespeare, and stresses somewhat more the personal feelings of the characters. At the end of one of the frequent truces, and on the "faire and cleere" day when the Trojans re-enter the field, Andromache begs her husband to refrain from combat.

> . . . this Andromeda sawe that night a maruellous vision, and her seemed if Hector went that day following to the battaile, he should be slaine. And she that had great feare and dread of her husband, weeping saide to him, praying him that he would not go to the battaile that day: whereof Hector blamed his wife, saying, that she shoulde not beleeue nor giue faith to dreames . . .
>   [Rec.II.610; AH, 526–27]

While Troilus and Aeneas issue into the field, and while Hector prepares to follow, Andromache hastens to Priam, who sends word that he is to stay in Troy.

> . . . Hector was angry, and said to his wife many wordes reprochful as he that knew well that this comandement came by her request, yet notwithstanding ye forbidding, he armed him . . . .   [Rec.II.611; AH, 527]

Priam, however, arrives in person, and forcibly stays Hector.

> . . . the king Priamus came running anon, and took him by the bridle, and said to him so many thinges of one and other, that hee made him to returne, but in no wise hee would vnarme him.[1]

When, however, Achilles slew Margareton, Hector "had great sorrow, and did anon lace on his helm, and went to the battaile, that his father knew not of" [Rec.II.612; AH, 528].[2]

---

1. Rec.II.611–12; AH, 528(in edition, 520).
2. Rec.II.612; AH, 528(in edition, 520).

HOMER

Chapman had not published Book VI of the Iliades in 1598.
Shakespeare could have read Hall's translation, but in his play
he has certainly not dramatized Homer's treatment of Hector
and Andromache. Yet in the epic, Hector will not be persuaded
by Andromache to withdraw his forces to a strategic spot. His
argument is that his death is fated, and a particular act will
not avert it.

Interestingly enough, in Book XXII, also untranslated by
Chapman in 1598, Priam and Hecuba plead with Hector to leave
the field when he stands alone with Achilles. But here he remains
adamant too.

> Thus wept both these, and to his ruth propos'd the
>   utmost worst
> Of what could chance them; yet he stay'd.
>
> [Iliads, II.xxii.76–77]

HEYWOOD

A combination of Homer and Caxton, even in the hands of Shakespeare, is not always a happy one: when Thomas Heywood is the
artificer, the combination is well-nigh disastrous. It is difficult to
believe that Heywood was not guilty of exaggeration when he observed
of his cycle of plays dealing with the Trojan war that they were
"often (and not with least applause,) Publickely Acted." To be sure,
he did not treat all the scenes that illustrate the history quite so
badly as that in which Hector takes leave of Andromache.

> Oh stay deare Lord, my royall husband stay,
> Cast by thy shield, fellow vncase his armes,
> Knock off the riuets, lay that baldricke by,
> But this one day rest with Andromache.
> . . . .
>   A fearefull dreame,
> This night me thought I saw thee 'mongst
>   the Greekes
> Round girt with squadrons of thine enemies,
> All which their Iauelins thrild against thy
>   brest,
> And stucke them in thy bosome.   [Dr.Wks. III.316]

After Paris makes a lewd jest, Hector attempts to dissuade his
wife from believing in dreams:

> Trust not deceptious visions, dreames are fables,
> Adulterate Sceanes of Anticke forgeries
> Playd vpon idle braines, come Lords to horse
> To keepe me from the field, dreames haue no force.
>
> [III.317]

Andromache, unable to move her husband, attempts to win him by
speaking of Astyanax, but Hector is only irked the more. "Helpe
to take off these burrs, they trouble mee" [Dr.Wks. III.317]. Paris
and Aeneas are able, however, to prevail on Hector to stay within
the gates. From the watchtower he views the battle, but, seeing
Achilles slay Margareton in the field below, he goes down to his
own death.

   In Troilus and Cressida Hector's assertion that he stands com-
mitted to enter the fight, having made a vow to the gods, is the
reason why he refuses to obey the entreaties of the women of Troy
and Priam's stern command. In the Troy Book,[3] and in the Recuyell,
Hector has no definite reason, no moral commitment, that binds
him to action even at the risk of his life. The mediaeval translators,
in their failure to put against Adromache's reason why he should
not enter the conflict, an adequate reason why he should, to over-
ride her objection, accomplished nothing more in the development
or revelation of character than to create in Hector an example of
unreasonable stubbornness.The unfortunate stigma that Lydgate and
Caxton place upon his character in this scene, Shakespeare wiped
off by making Hector adhere to a definite principle, even though it
proves to be one favored neither by the gods nor by the women.
   By motivating Hector's conduct, by giving him a justifiable reason
for combatting the logic of Priam, the seeming phantasy of Cassandra,
and the dream of Andromache, Shakespeare strengthened Hector's
character as a protagonist, as an agent in this scene. He is a match
for the emotional women. He is not the stubborn, fretful, and finally
yielding character he is in the earlier accounts.
   In this scene as handled by Lydgate and Caxton, Troilus has no
part in the action. He is already afield with Aeneas. In the Iron Age,
on the other hand, Troilus is with Hector when he is besieged by
the women of Troy. But he takes no part in the conversation. He
makes no attempt to influence Hector's decision. Shakespeare developed Troilus' position in this scene, as far as can be determined,
without a suggestion from his predecessors. He saw fit to introduce
him as a dramatic contrast to Hector's character and position. The
conversation between the brothers reveals that Hector's behaviour
in maintaining the ethic of fair play (against which Troilus advises
him) is an extension of that moral principle which will not allow him
to compromise a vow to an emotional appeal.
   Shakespeare intentionally omitted from his play reference to
Hector's children, since he could not overlook their presence in
the Recuyell or in the Troy Book. For his purpose, of course, Priam,
Andromache, and Cassandra were foils enough for Hector's character at this period in the action.

----

3. See Appendix I, v, for pertinent passages.

Shakespeare retained, however, a few details from the earlier versions. Hector's rough words to Andromache, though they are mollified in the drama, he adapted from Caxton, or possibly from Lydgate. Andromache's dream is substantially the same in all accounts. Cassandra, whose importance in the play is considerable, is not mentioned as present by Caxton, though in the Troy Book she is numbered among the women who attempt, as a collective group, to prevail upon Hector to do as they desire.[4]

One might think that Cassandra's presence in this account would be evidence that Shakespeare was at least in one instance more indebted to Lydgate than to Caxton. But when we consider that Shakespeare introduces Cassandra in the Trojan scenes when a fateful decision is imminent, acceptance of coincidence seems to be nearer the truth than the assumption of Shakespeare's specific debt to Lydgate.

In developing the last meeting between Hector and Andromache, Shakespeare was doubtless indebted to Caxton for the substance of the scene. But the treatment is Shakespeare's own. He definitely re-wrote it with the purpose of strengthening the character of Hector and also with the idea in mind of linking this scene to the action that had gone before. The pledge he and Achilles made in Act IV, scene v, has a definite effect on governing the action of Hector in this scene. By keeping him alert to his pledge and making that the touchstone of his action, Shakespeare united this episode to the one that had gone before.

As we have noted, Shakespeare treated the scene between Hector and Andromache in a way that shows no familiarity with the well-known Homeric situation, except that Hector does not yield to entreaty. Later in the action when he is sued to by his father and mother he still remains adamant. Homer's and Shakespeare's Hector have this firmness of purpose in common—yet the books of the Iliad in which this trait of Hector's nature is stressed were not then available in Chapman's translation. If Homer is the source of this inspiration, then Shakespeare read some of the Iliad not translated.

9. The Death of Patroclus

SHAKESPEARE

The time that elapses from the day on which the action of the play begins until Achilles slays Hector cannot be measured with complete accuracy. Commentators have noted discrepancies and contradictions in the time sequence of the drama.[1] The Chorus informs the spectator that the action of the play opens during the middle of the siege.

4. Troy Book, III.5074. "With whom was . . . hir suster Cassandra."
1. Troilus and Cressida, Intro. pp. xxx ff.

> . . . our play
> Leap's o'er the vaunt and firstlings of those broils,
> Beginning in the middle . . . .   [Prologue, 26–28]

In Act I, scene iii, Agamemnon speaks of the present time as being
the seventh year of the Greek siege: "after seven years' siege yet
Troy walls stand" [I.iii.12]. Aeneas, as soon as the Greek council
has diagnosed the infirmity of the command, enters the enemy
camp to offer Hector's challenge. The combat, we are informed on
several occasions, is to take place on the following day. Hector

> will to-morrow with his trumpet call,
> Midway between your tents and walls of Troy.
>   [I.iii.276–77]

Achilles reports the substance of the challenge to Ajax:

> That Hector, by the fifth hour of the sun,
> Will with a trumpet 'twixt our tents and Troy
> To-morrow morning call some knight to arms . . . .
>   [II.i.132–34]
> Now shall we see to-morrow,—
> An act that very chance doth throw upon him,—
> Ajax renown'd.   [III.iii.130–32]

The same day that the combat takes place, Hector visits the Greek
camp. There Achilles tells his opponent that he will meet him in
combat on the following day: "To-morrow do I meet thee fell as
death" [IV.v.269]. That same evening, while he awaits Hector's
visit to his own tent, Achilles tells Patroclus:

> I'll heat his blood with Greekish wine to-night,
> Which with my scimitar I'll cool to-morrow. [V.i.1–2]

That very night, however, Achilles receives a letter from Hecuba
instructing him not to break the vow he formerly made to perform
no hostile act against Troy [V.i.41 ff.]. The action of the following
scene, in which Troilus learns that Cressida, like her father, has
allied herself with the Greek cause, takes place the same night the
Trojan leaders are guests of the Greeks. Aeneas late that night
seeks out Troilus to guide him back to Troy:

> I have been seeking you this hour, my lord.
> Hector, by this, is arming him in Troy:
> Ajax, your guard, stays to conduct you home.
>   [V.ii.178–80]

In Act V, scene iii, Hector is armed for combat to fulfill his vow
to the gods that he will fight those to whom he is pledged in faith.
Achilles is, of course, one of the Greeks to whom he stands engaged.
He and Achilles had grasped hands the day before to bind their
intent to fight the combat [V.v.270]. Hector, however, isn't aware
that Achilles has broken his pledge [V.i.41 ff.]. In the following

scene, the long truce is ended[2] by general combat and, as far as can be determined, the battle is continuous from that period to the death of Hector. In the first battle scene, Diomedes and Troilus are the principal contestants [V. v.]. In scene v, which is a part of the same general action, "Another part of the field" in the words of the eighteenth century stage direction, Patroclus, we learn from Agamemnon, is either captured by the enemy or slain. The general slaughter is so great that observance of the fate of a particular hero is obscure [V. v. 13].

Nestor, a few minutes later, has a clearer picture of what has happened in the great melee. It is through his words we learn of Patroclus' certain death. "Go, bear Patroclus' body to Achilles" [V. v. 17]. In a different scene, but during the same battle, Hector is slain by Achilles.

Though the many incidents of the play give the impression of protracted action, in reality the action takes place in three or at most four days. By Shakespeare's calculation, Hector was slain in the seventh year of the siege, and the Homeric Ten Years' War is reduced by three years. The impression is, however, that Patroclus is slain at a much later date, though not long before Hector.

CAXTON

According to Diomedes, one year passed from the date the Greek fleet arrived at Tenedos to the day when he urged his colleagues to leave in order to begin the siege of Troy before the Trojans had more time to fortify their city and gain more allies from the surrounding country.

> . . . all ye Kinges, Princes and Barons, that be here assembled, we ought to haue great shame and dislike, seeing it is a yeare agone since we landed heere in this countrey, and haue not yet been before Troy. Verily, in this we haue giuen to our enemies great aduantage . . . .
> [Rec.II.569; AH, 490]

"On the morrowe early," the Greek host, mindful of Diomedes' wisdom, departs from Tenedos and on the same day engages the enemy in the first battle. By evening, the Greeks are in possession of a strip of the Trojan plain where they spend the night. Those who had "no tentes nor pauilions, lodged them vnder the leaues, the best wise that they could . . . and their horses" [Rec.II.575; AH, 496]. In Troy, "when the night was passed" [Ibid.], Hector, who had charge of all the battalions, assembled them "in a great plaine, that was in the Citie" [Ibid.] and appointed a warrior to lead each battalion.

2. Antenor, according to Calchas (III.iii.18–19), was "Yesterday took" prisoner, a contradiction to Hector's words about the long truce (I.iii.261).

Once they are assembled and armed for conflict, Hector leads them into the field to begin the second battle, which, as far as the text indicates, begins on the day after the Greeks made their initial and successful landing on the Trojan coast.

In the meantime Agamemnon had not been "idle." He had "ordeined his battels," and had appointed Patroclus to lead the first battalion, ordinarily Achilles' battalion; but on the second day of the battle, it is under Patroclus' command, since the Myrmidon chief is suffering from wounds sustained in the initial landing. "He [Agamemnon] put in the first battell Patroclus with his people, & with them the folke of Achilles, which was not that day in the battell, for his wounds that he had, and did stay to heale them in his tent . . . ." [Rec.II. 578-79; AH, 499].

The second battle is fierce, and during the day Patroclus is slain by Hector, on the second day of the siege.

> When all the battels were set in order on the one side and on the other, and there was nothing to do but to meet, then aduaunced him Hector all the first, and Patroclus came against him, as fast as his horse might runne, and smote him so strongly with his speare on his shield, that he pearsed it thorowe out, but more harme did it not. Then Hector assailed Patroclus with his sworde, and gaue him so great a stroke vpon his head, that he cleft it in two pieces: and Patroclus fell downe dead to the ground.
> [Rec.II.580; AH, 500; Troy Book: App. I.vi]

HOMER

In the Iliades, Patroclus is slain by Hector near the end of the ninth year of the Trojan war. Ulysses had stated before the assemblage, when revolt was rife throughout the host, and the desire to return to the homeland was paramount to the desire for glory and victory, that the Delphic oracle had prophesied a Ten Years' War, the ninth and last being now [pp. 29-30]. Considerable action takes place and time passes from the day Ulysses makes his plea to the Greeks until the day Patroclus lies slain by Hector.

In the eighteenth book of the Iliades, which Chapman published in 1598 under the title of Achilles Shield, Thetis describes Patroclus' death.

> He [Achilles] deckt his dear Patroclus in his armes
> And sent him with his handes to those debates:
> All daye they fought before the Scaean gates
> And well might haue expugnde, by that black light,
> The Ilian Cittie, if Apollos spight,
> Thirsting the blood of good Menetius sonne:
> Had not in face of all the fight foredone
> His faultlesse life; and authord the renowne
> Of Hectors prowesse, making th' act his owne:
> Since therefore, to reuenge the timeless death
> Of his true friend, my sonne determineth
> T'embrue the field . . . .   [pp. 4-5]

HEYWOOD

The entire action of the Trojan legend which Shakespeare unfolded
in five acts, Heywood in the Iron Age compressed within Acts II, III,
and IV. It is not possible to determine with accuracy the time sequence
of the Iron Age, since Heywood has no reference to the lapse of time.
But by comparing the order of events in the play with the order in
the Caxton or Lydgate version, though Heywood made alterations and
additions, the events can be paralleled with reasonable enough accuracy to gain an estimate of time sequence. In such a reckoning, Patroclus' death seems to occur late in the siege. In the last scene of
the third act, Patroclus is slain, Hector at the beginning of the
fourth.
    While Achilles plays the idler in his tent, amidst the holocaust
around him, Patroclus, with Achilles' permission, takes the Myrmidons into the field. Both they and he fare very badly indeed before
Hector's onslaughts.

> Alarum. Enter Diomed wounded, bringing in
> Patroclus dying.
>
> Dio. Looke here Achilles.
> Achi. Patroclus?
> Pat. This wound great Hector gaue:
> Reuenge my death, before I meete my graue.
>   [Dr.Wks. III.312–13]

But still Achilles does not enter the battle until the Trojans actually
set fire to his tent [III.314].

    Shakespeare was indebted to Book XVIII of the Iliades for his de-
scription of the death of Patroclus, and for its place in the general
action. Though one cannot ascertain from Heywood's play exactly
at what stage of the war Patroclus was slain, Lydgate and Caxton
are explicit in assigning his fateful appearance against Hector to
the day after the Greeks first landed on the Trojan plain. Since the
Greeks had tarried for one year at Tenedos, and Patroclus died
during the second battle on Trojan soil, his death occurred during
the second year of the expedition or during the first year of the
siege of Troy. According to Homer, who is concerned with events
of the last year of the war, Patroclus was slain late in the ninth
year, since Achilles, as soon as he receives new armor, takes up
the fight against Hector which, according to Thetis, means not only
the doom of Troy but his own end as well. Though Shakespeare
assigns Patroclus' death to the seventh year, that is by reckoning
the time sequence in the drama closely, the impression is that Patroclus meets his death at the very end of the siege. At any rate,
Hector does not live long after Patroclus is slain.
    It is therefore patent that Shakespeare departed from Caxton in
his conception of happenings during the siege of Troy. In the general

sequence of events, Patroclus' death occurs at relatively the same
time that it does in the Iliades, and in a situation analogous to that
in the epic. In the drama, epic, and in Heywood's play, in contra-
distinction to the narratives, Patroclus plays a part in the action
and lives until the last year or years of the siege. Homer was unquestionably Shakespeare's guide in the conception of this episode,
as he was generally his guide in the selection of situations that
constitute the action of the siege plot. In the mediaeval accounts,
on the other hand, Patroclus' importance is confined to the effect
his early death has on Achilles' memory.

But as a dramatic character, Patroclus plays a small part, even
though he is present off and on during the action. Shakespeare has
not developed him to a greater extent than to make him serve as an
example of an insubordinate leader, and as an hindrance to Achilles.
In Chapman's account there was little for the dramatist to work
upon. What there was Shakespeare made use of to point up his theme.

10. The Letter from Hecuba

SHAKESPEARE

On the day Hector visits the Grecian camp, Ulysses has reason
to believe his carefully planned stratagem to arouse Achilles has
been a success. Achilles, who witnessed with scorn "the maiden
battle" between Hector and Ajax, who saw Hector unarmed, and
viewed him limb by limb to determine in what part of his body to
make the fatal thrust, is inclined to show Hector what a battle with
him will be like.

> To-morrow do I meet thee, fell as death;
> To-night all friends.   [IV.v.269–70]

Later the same day, while he awaits Hector's presence in his tent,
Achilles remarks to Patroclus,

> I'll heat his blood with Greekish wine to-night,
> Which with my scimitar I'll cool to-morrow.   [V.i.1–2]

On the evening of the same day, the spectator learns, however,
that Achilles' passion for battle, which the outcome of the stratagem aroused, suddenly abates, before his emotional response passes
into physical activity. The dramatist introduces what almost amounts
to a deus ex machina in the form of a letter from Queen Hecuba
who begs the Myrmidon leader to refrain from any hostile act
against Troy or any Trojan. The Achilles who has been primed to
fight by Ulysses' carefully planned stratagem is undone by the
more amorous Achilles who follows the dictates of the enemy queen.

> My sweet Patroclus, I am thwarted quite
> From my great purpose in to-morrow's battle.
> Here is a letter from Queen Hecuba,

A token from her daughter, my fair love,
Both taxing me and gaging me to keep
An oath that I have sworn. I will not break it:
Fall, Greeks; fail, fame; honour or go or stay;
My major vow lies here, this I'll obey.   [V.i.41–48]

Though Achilles keeps his vow to the queen, he has no scruple about breaking his pledge with Hector to fight with him on the morrow.

CAXTON

In the Recuyell, Hector has been dead for more than one year when Achilles is so sorely afflicted with love for his sister [Rec. II.618 ff.; AH, 533 ff.]. Though the battle at this time during the action is fierce and sharp, it is neither fiercer nor sharper than the passion which possesses Achilles within, and which will not allow him to succor his own forces that are being hacked by Troilus' sword. The message which Achilles receives from Queen Hecuba differs from the letter Shakespeare's Achilles receives. Caxton's Hecuba demands that Achilles, if he expects to win Polyxena as wife, shall establish peace between the two armies. The messenger relays this information to Achilles.

> . . . I haue spoken to my husband, and also to my sonne
> Paris of the request, and also of the promise of thy Lord:
> and they be content that this his re-request be agreed to him:
> so as, that he do first that thing that hee hath promised:
> and so thou maiest say to him, that hee may come to the
> chiefe and end of his desire, if that he conduct wisely and
> secretly this thing asmuch as in him is.
>   [Rec.II.623–24; AH, 540/538 (so in edition)]

Achilles is not aware that the Greeks will suffer any loss of honor if the bargain of peace is sealed.

> . . . and it ought to suffise to vs that we haue nowe slaine
> Hector and many other of their nobles, by the which we might
> now returne with our honour and worship . . . .
>   [Rec.II.625; AH, 541/539 (so in edition)]

HEYWOOD

In the Iron Age, in which Achilles' love for Polyxena is presented in greater detail than it is in Troilus and Cressida, Achilles on two different occasions receives missives from Hecuba. The first message is delivered by Aeneas before Hector is slain. It causes Achilles' withdrawal from battle.

> Aene. Behold Queene Hecubaes hand, King Priams
>   seale,
> With the consent of faire Polixena,
> Condition'd thus, Achilles shall forbare
> To dammage Troy.

> Achi. Returne this answere backe,
> Tell Priam that Achilles Arme's benumb'd,
> And cannot lift a weapon against Troy.
>
> [Dr.Wks. III.310]

Achilles breaks his vow to refrain from battle when the Trojans
set fire to his tent. Then he takes up arms and slays Hector. This
broken vow, however, Hecuba forgives, though she sends a second
missive urging him to fight no more.

> Vlisses, here's a Briefe from Hecuba,
> Wherein shee vowes, if I but kill one Troian,
> I neuer shall inioy Polixena.   [III.324]

An analysis of the letter that Achilles receives from Hecuba reveals that in Troilus and Cressida the contents are different from
the words the messenger brings from Troy in either the Troy Book
(see Appendix I, vii) or in the Recuyell. In the earlier versions,
Hecuba demands that Achilles fulfill the vow he swore to perform
in exchange for Polyxena: namely the establishment of peace between
the Greek and Trojan armies. Achilles is the author of this fantastic
proposal; Hecuba merely insists that he perform his promise. In
Shakespeare's account, there is no mention of a general peace as
a stipulation in the love-suit. Hecuba demands that Achilles cease
from all hostile action if he hopes to win Polyxena as his wife.
Strictly speaking, the communication between the Myrmidon chief
and the Trojan queen in the early versions is carried out by a
messenger: in the play, by letter.

Heywood's treatment of the incident is closer to Shakespeare's
interpretation. Though Aeneas bears the first sealed letter to
Achilles, its contents demand that Achilles shall not damage Troy:
in the second letter Hecuba vows that if he kills but one more Trojan, he shall never enjoy her daughter.

The idea of the message obviously comes from one of the early
versions of the siege, and the similarity in the contents of the
letters in the two plays is striking. And that both dramatists dropped
from their plays the demand of a general peace as a condition in
the fulfillment of the love-suit, is no less striking. If one dramatist
was indebted to the other, Heywood was very likely the borrower.

Though Heywood's Achilles has no thought of any personal or
communal honor involved in his decision to satisfy his passion,
Shakespeare's Achilles does not accept his position entirely without remorse or realization of the loss of honor and fame his decision will exact. "Fall, Greeks; fail fame; honour or go or stay;
my major vow lies here." His attitude is unlike that of the Achilles
Lydgate and Caxton depicted who can see no loss of honor or merit
in the decision to make peace. Though the episode in itself does
not raise one's esteem of Achilles, at least in his reaction to it
there is an intimation of some nobility of character.

It is more likely that Shakespeare took the idea of the message from Caxton than from Lydgate, though he entirely refashioned it. It acts in the drama as a deterrent to Achilles' desire for combat, for which the outcome of Ulysses' plan successfully primed him. The deus ex machina in the form of a letter does not appear to be an entirely happy introduction since it makes the carefully planned stratagem seem purposeless.

But from an Elizabethan spectator's point of view (if one can hazard an explanation of it), this sudden and unprepared development in the action, which threatens a second crisis in Achilles' relation to the Greek command, would not appear undesirable. Scholars have pointed out that the sudden turn of an event in an Elizabethan play was frequently more appreciated than a logical and expected action.[1] The letter incident as it stands in Troilus and Cressida is an indication of Shakespeare's fidelity to current dramatic methods to obtain an effect.

Until the combat, expectation was centered on the outcome of Ulysses' plan. It seemed entirely to misfire when Achilles made no response to the fight between Ajax and Hector. But suddenly Achilles' blood lust was aroused by recollection of "the maiden battle" and the sight of Hector in his weeds of peace. With the promise of "To-morrow do I meet thee, fell as death," the audience is primed to witness the long delayed combat between the great contenders. But the course of the drama suddenly takes a turn aside, and expectation for the fight is suddenly checked. An unforseen conflict has arisen.

It has been observed that the material Shakespeare was working up into the drama was static, relatively inactive in nature. He used the challenge, stratagem, and combat with great skill in order to simulate an air of activity and suspense though there was little action. Now the introduction of the letter was unquestionably for the purpose of arousing further suspense at a place in the drama when all events promised to run smoothly to their foregone conclusion. In a play composed of great talkers and not mighty doers (at this time of the siege), one might suppose Shakespeare would make use of an incident that would create a stir. Whatever one might think of the episode in itself, the reason for its presence in the drama is clear enough, and it is no doubt not ineffective as "good theater."

11. Motives for the Return of Achilles

SHAKESPEARE

Throughout Troilus and Cressida, Achilles remains aloof from activity in the field and in council. He keeps to his tent. There is no change in his position. His emotions, however, are less stable

1. Elmer E. Stoll, Art and Artifice in Shakespeare (Cambridge, 1938), p. 56.

than the position he maintains. From the moment Ulysses puts
his stratagem in practice a perceptible alteration in Achilles' attitude towards his own position becomes noticeable. After Ulysses
has revealed to him that the "golden opinion" he once possessed
is now lost, and is the possession of another far less worthy, A-
chilles becomes less certain of the wisdom of his own stand. On
the evening when Hector visits the Grecian camp, Achilles is prepared, emotionally, to take up arms against him. While he has remained physically inactive, he has undergone a gradual emotional
change. "To-morrow do I meet thee, fell as death," he tells Hector.
The letter he receives from Hecuba suddenly frustrates him. He
obeys its injunctions; but his reaction is that of a man who is emotionally aroused. He is primed for action; only temporarily checked.
   Shakespeare skillfully prepared the way for Achilles' return to
combat by preparing his mind for that event. It is an accumulative
process; it receives checks; but the dramatist carefully built up
the emotional change Achilles' character undergoes from the time
he first appears in Act I until he makes a final appearance in Act V.
   When Patroclus' body is brought to his tent, and he sees returning from the field his badly defeated Myrmidons, Achilles' emotions,
earlier stimulated by Ulysses' words and ideas, and more recently
aroused by the combat and the sight of Hector, find sudden release
in revengeful activity on the battle-field. Vows and checks that he
heeded the night before cannot stem the sudden and violent release
of his passion.

> O! courage, courage, princes; great Achilles
> Is arming, weeping, cursing, vowing vengeance:
> Patroclus' wounds have rous'd his drowsy blood,
> Together with his mangled Myrmidons,
> That noseless, handless, hack'd and chipp'd,
>   come to him,
> Crying on Hector.   [V. v. 30-35]

   The portrait of Achilles as an exemplum of perturbation is further
rounded by this description of Achilles in a tempest and whirlwind
of passion.

CAXTON

   In the Recuyell, Achilles' withdrawal from combat occurs after
Hector has been slain; one year after, to be exact. Patroclus has
been dead a much longer time, having been slain on the second day
of the war while the Greeks were establishing their positions on
the fringe of the Trojan plain. Troilus has taken over Hector's
place as the mainstay of Troy at the time Achilles withdraws from
action, although the new Trojan leader duplicates the havoc his
late brother inflicted on the Greeks.
   Achilles, in spite of the entreaties of the Greek councilors, will
not return to the field, although he consents to lend to Agamemnon

his Myrmidons to aid the ever-weakening Greek defense. ". . . for-
asmuch as he loued Agamenon, he agreed and consented yt his men
should go to battel without him . . . and Achilles sent to him his
Mirmidones clad & marked with a red signe, for to be knowen."
[Rec.II.634; AH, 547].

In the sixteenth battle of the war, Troilus "ceased not to grieue
the Mirmidones, and there was none so puissaunt, nor so strong,
that might endure against him, and hee did so much, that hee put
the greeks to flight . . ." [Rec.II.635; AH, 548]. Achilles, still scrupulous in keeping the terms of his vow, restrains his anger until the
eighteenth battle begins. On that disastrous day, the Trojan forces
enter the Grecian camp, and slay the Greeks in their own tents.
The Myrmidons suffer too keenly for Achilles to ignore their plight.

> . . . and [Troilus] did so much, that he made the Greekes to
> go backe into their Tentes, and alighted on foote and entered
> into the tentes, and slewe them on all sides: and there was
> so great a crie, that the sounde came to Achilles, that rested
> him in his Tent, and demaunded of one of his seruauntes that
> was there, what it was? and he said to him; that the Troyans
> had vanquished the Greekes, and slewe them within their
> Tents, which were no more able to defend them: and thinke
> ye to be sure here said he:? nay ye shall see anon more then
> forty thousand Troyans that shall slea you vnarmed: for at
> this time they haue slaine the most part of your Mirmidones,
> and they cease not to slea them, and there shall not abide
> one aliue, but if they be succoured.
> At these wordes Achilles did quake for yre, and set behinde
> him the loue of Polixene, and did arme him hastily, and
> mounted on his horse, and ranne all out enraged as a Lion,
> and smote in among the Troyans, and spoiled thẽ, slewe and
> hurt them in such wise, that anon his sworde was knowne,
> and the bloud ran in the field and all about as he went.
>   [Rec.II.636-37; AH,549-50]

In the Caxton version of the siege, Patroclus' death does not
arouse Achilles to instant revenge against Hector. Considerable
time elapses between the first death and the second. When Achilles
does meet and slay Hector, the incident is one of many in a general
action [Rec.II.612 ff.; AH, 529].

HOMER

In Achilles Shield (Chapman's translation of the eighteenth book
of the Iliad), Thetis describes Achilles' reaction to Patroclus' death.

> . . . to reuenge the timelesse death
> Of his true friend, my sonne determineth
> T'embrue the field; for want whereof he lies
> Buried in dust, and drownde in miseries.   [p. 5]

As soon as Vulcan can furnish new arms, Achilles returns to combat
to atone with the blood of the slayer for the death of his friend.

HEYWOOD

The fate of Patroclus does not incite Heywood's Achilles to take
instant revenge on Hector. Ajax reminds Achilles, as he stares un-
moved at Patroclus' body,

> Had I lost Patroclus, a deere friend
> As thou hast done, I would haue dond these armes
> In which he dyed, sprung through the Troian hoast,
> And mauger opposition, let the blow
> Or by the same hand dy'd . . . .   [Dr.Wks.III.313]

This plea does not move Achilles. He is driven to action only by
the devastating presence of armed Trojans in the Grecian camp,
burning and slaying armed as well as unarmed men they find in
the tents. Literally, as Ajax says, Achilles is "fired out" and driven
to act to defend his life.

> Aga. Doth no man aske where is this double fire,
> That two wayes flyes towards heauen?
> Vpon the right our royall Nauy burnes,
> Vpon the left Achilles Tents on fire.
>
> Achi. Our Tent?
>
> Aga. By Ioue thy Tent . . .
>
> Achi. My sword and armour:
> Polixena, thy loue we will lay by,
> Till by this hand, that Troian Hector dye.   [III.313 ff.]

When Achilles encounters Hector, he has more reasons than Patroclus' death for slaying him.

> That shall my Launce
> In bloody letters text vpon thy breast,
> For young Patroclus death, for my dishonours,
> For thousand spoyles, and for that infinite wracke
> Our army hath indur'd onely by thee,
> Thy life must yeeld me satisfaction.   [III.321]

Professor Campbell writes thus in discussing Achilles' return
to combat: "Reason cannot bring him back to his social obligations.
Only when the killing of Patroclus arouses in him a tempest of
grief and rage does he return to battle. Then he acts, not like a
soldier obeying the rules of warfare, but like a man insane with
rage; so failure overtakes Ulysses' nicely devised plan to induce
this Olympian school-boy to obey the dictates of self-interest as
rationalized and implemented by a social ideal. The outcome, as
in the case of all the other efforts of the characters, whether
reasonable or irrational, is futility, and was meant to awaken
scornful laughter." [1]

1. O. J. Campbell, Comicall Satyre and Shakespeare's Troilus
and Cressida (San Marino, 1938), p. 201.

It is very doubtful if the outcome of the actions and efforts of the characters in the play would awaken scornful laughter. There is nothing inherently comic or satiric in any of the incidents so far discussed. In the second place, Ulysses' "nicely devised plan" is no failure. It does succeed in preparing Achilles for combat. He is eager to meet and kill Hector after he witnesses the "maiden battle," and sees Hector in his "weeds of peace." He will show Hector what a combat with him will be like. "To-morrow do I meet thee, fell as death." Hecuba's letter, though it checks his purpose, is not an instance of that kind of frustration that is the butt of comical satire. In part, it is an instance of contemporary dramatic technique (see above Section 10), perhaps not skillfully handled in this instance by Shakespeare, and though the letter episode does round out the picture of a confused Achilles ("My mind is troubled like a fountain stirr'd, / And I myself see not the bottom of it"), the frustration, it seems to me, is not of the quality that causes laughter.

Shakespeare's fierce figure who enters the battle "not like a soldier obeying the rules of warfare, but like a man insane with rage," is Chapman's conception of the hero of the ancient epic. In play and poem, Achilles is drawn as an exemplum of perturbation of spirit resulting from excessive passion. Humanists with Sidney's outlook on the arts would surely place a plaudit on the dramatist's consistent and well-worked-out portrait of Achilles.

In motivating his return to action, Shakespeare was indebted to Homer alone. Only in the epic and in the play does Patroclus' death arouse Achilles to instant action. Hector does not live long after Patroclus is slain. In the histories of Lydgate[2] and Caxton, on the other hand, Patroclus has been dead for years, and when Achilles takes up arms, he does so for other reasons, though he has not forgotten Patroclus. In the Iron Age, Achilles returns to combat because the Trojans fire his tent. Obviously Shakespeare was following the Homeric pattern in which Patroclus was a participator with Achilles nearly to the end of the war.

A second motive for Achilles' return which Shakespeare introduced, though not the primary one, namely, the slaughter of the Myrmidons, he transferred most likely from Caxton. But in his version (as well as in Lydgate's), the slaughter of his army drives him to action at a different time. Hector has long since been dead; Troilus is the new Hector. If Shakespeare made use of Caxton, he transferred this motive from the Troilus-Achilles situation to the Hector-Achilles situation. Doubtless the addition is purposeful; for by it, Shakespeare emphasizes the magnitude of the battle, and the formidable character of Hector as holder-up of Troy.

---

2. See Appendix I, viii for pertinent passages in the Troy Book.

12. *The Death of Hector*

SHAKESPEARE

In the last act of <u>Troilus and Cressida</u>, the first armed encounter between Achilles and Hector does not develop into a combat. Though Achilles is in the field to avenge Patroclus' death by slaying Hector, when he meets the Trojan leader, he forgoes the fight, out of weariness. Hector feels that he himself isn't as fresh as he should be to match arms against Achilles.

> <u>Achil.</u> Now do I see thee. Ha! have at thee,
>   Hector!
> <u>Hect.</u> Pause, if thou wilt.
>
> <u>Achil.</u> I do disdain thy courtesy, proud Trojan.
> Be happy that my arms are out of use:
> My rest and negligence befriend thee now,
> But thou anon shalt hear of me again;
> Till when, go seek thy fortune.   [Exit]
>
> <u>Hect.</u> . . . .
> I would have been much more a fresher man,
> Had I expected thee.   [V. vi.13–21]

In the following scene, Achilles instructs his Myrmidons in the manner of slaying Hector. Presumably, this scene takes place at a later date in the day, or more likely on a different day, since Achilles is ready to seek and slay Hector.

> Come here about me, you my Myrmidons;
> Mark what I say. Attend me where I wheel:
> Strike not a stroke, but keep yourselves
>   in breath:
> And when I have the bloody Hector found,
> Empale him with your weapons round about;
> In fellest manner execute your aims.
> Follow me . . . .   [V. vii.1–7]

In another part of the field, Hector is stripping a corpse of its "goodly armour" when Achilles suddenly confronts him.

> <u>Achil.</u> Look, Hector, how the sun begins to set;
> How ugly night comes breathing at his heels:
> Even with the vail and darking of the sun,
> To close the day up, Hector's life is done.
> <u>Hect.</u> I am unarm'd; forgo this vantage, Greek.
> <u>Achil.</u> Strike, fellows, strike this is the man
>   I seek.   [Hector falls.]
> . . . .
> Come, tie his body to my horse's tail;
> Along the field I will the Trojan trail.   [V. viii.5–22]

CAXTON

In the Recuyell, the Greeks have no hope of success while Hector lives. He must be slain at all costs. Agamemnon summons his councilors for a special meeting, and delegates Achilles to be the man to slay Hector, since he alone has both the strength and the wisdom to achieve victory over him.

> After this battaile, when the night was come, all the kings, princes and barons of the Greekes assembled at the Tent of king Agamemnon, and there held they their parliament howe they might slea Hector. And they said, that as long as hee were aliue, and came to battaile against them, they might neuer vanquish the Troyans: but he should to them doe great damage. And for to bring this thing to the end, they requested Achilles, that hee woulde take it vppon him, as well for his strength as for his wisedome. And Achilles enterprised it gladly . . . .   [Rec.II.594; AH, 512]

Achilles is not able to slay Hector at once. He has several fierce encounters with him, but has neither the strength nor the wisdom to compass his death. Achilles finally achieves victory by slaying Hector when he is unarmed.

> Among all these things, Hector had taken a very noble baron of Greece, that was queintly and richly armed, and for to leade him out of the hoste at his ease, had cast his shielde behinde him at his backe, and had left his breast discouereed: and as hee was in this point, and tooke none heede of Achilles, he came priuily vnto him, and thrust his speare within his bodie, and Hector fell downe dead to the grounde . . . for the death of Hector, were al the Troyans discomfited, and reentred into their citie, bearing the bodie of Hector with great sorrow and lamentation.
> [Rec.II.613–14; AH, 529]

HOMER

Though the twenty-second book of the Iliad was not translated into English when Troilus and Cressida was written, it is necessary to consider Homer's description of Hector's death, since there is a similarity of treatment in the epic and in the drama.
When Achilles has driven Hector four times about the town,

> Then Jove his golden scales weigh'd up, and took the
>   last accounts
> Of fate for Hector, putting in for him and Peleus' son
> Two fates of bitter death, of which high heav'n
>   receiv'd the one,
> The other hell; so low declin'd the light of Hector's
>   life.   [Iliads, ed. Hooper, xxii.180 ff.]

Athene, "like Deiphobus in shape and voice," persuades Hector to stand and fight Achilles.

> O brother, thou art too much urg'd to be thus
>   combated
> About our own walls; let us stand, and force to
>   a retreat
> Th' insulting chaser.   [II.xxii.196 ff.]

When Hector casts his lance, which fails to penetrate Achilles' armour, and calls on Deiphobus for another, neither lance nor Deiphobus is at hand. Hector draws his sword, but Achilles first finds the "way to his thirsted life."

>   Of all ways, only one
> Appear'd to him, and that was where th' unequal
>   winding bone,
> That joins the shoulders and the neck, had place,
>   and where there lay
> The speeding way to death; and there his quick eye
>   could display
> The place it sought, e'en through those arms his
>   friend Patrolcus wore
> When Hector slew him. There he aim'd, and there
>   his jav'lin tore
> Stern passage quite through Hector's neck. [II.xxii.277 ff.]

Hector slain, Achilles

> . . . a work not worthy him he set to; of both feet
> He bor'd the nerves through from the heel to th'
>   ankle, and then knit
> Both to his chariot with a thong of whitleather,
>   his head
> Trailing the centre. Up he got to chariot, where
>   he laid
> The arms repurchas'd, and scourg'd on his horse
>   that freely flew.   [II.xxii.399 ff.]

Though Hector is not engaged at the point of death in stripping a knight of armor, his covetousness for the shield of Nestor, and the "Curace" of Diomed is alluded to by Homer. He urges his men redouble blows

>   . . . that we may take for prise
> The shield of old Nelcides, which Fame euen to the
>   skyes,
> Reports to be of gold informd, with handles all of
>   gold:
> And from the shoulders let vs take, of Diomede the
>   bold,
> The royall Curace Vulcan wrought, with art so
>   exquisite . . . .   [Iliades, p. 64]

HEYWOOD

In the Iron Age, Hector is not slain while engaged in the task of stripping a richly clothed knight of his armour. He is in the field,

despite Priam's command that he stay in Troy, to slay Achilles
for having slain Margareton. There, however, he meets more than
Achilles: he meets Achilles "with his guard of Mermidons."

> Achil. Come cast your selues into a ring of
>   terrour,
> And this warlike Prince, by whom I bleede.
>
> Hect. What meanes the glory of the Grecian
>   hoast
> Thus to besiege me with his Mermidons?
> And keepe aloofe himselfe.   [Dr.Wks. III.321]

Hector puts up a brave fight against so many adversaries.

> Come your slaues,
> Before I fall, Ile make some food for graues,
> That gape to swallow cowards . . . .   [III.322]

There are, however, too many Myrmidons for Hector to rout.
He "fals slayne by the Mirmidons, then Achilles wounds him with
his Lance." Though Achilles has respect for his spirit, he has none
for his body.

> Farwel the noblest spirit that ere breath'd
> In any terrene mansion: Take vp his body
> And beare it to my Tent: Ile straight to horse,
> And at his fetlockes to my greater glory,
> Ile dragge his mangled trunke that Grecians all,
> May deafe the world with shouts, at Hectors fall.[III.322]

Shakespeare combined elements from several different sources
to portray Hector's death. In the Recuyell, Agamemnon delegates
Achilles, because of his great strength and wisdom, to dispatch
Hector with all possible speed. The method Achilles favors is not
told in the council scene. Lydgate, describing the same situation
(see Appendix I, ix, for excerpts), makes it clear that the councilors
prefer Achilles to accomplish the deed by trickery, or by catching
him off his guard. In fair fight, Achilles' chance of victory may be
less certain.

> . . . thei gan to conspire blive
> The deth of hym, in many sondry woye,
>
> . . . .
> That be som sleight of a-wait lying,
> When he were most besy in fightynge,
> Amongis hem in meschef or distresse,
> That Achilles do his besynes. [Troy Book, III.2690 ff.]

In the play, there is no comparable scene. But Achilles does have
a plan to slay Hector. He delegates the task to the Myrmidons who
will "Empale him" with their weapons, and "in fellest manner execute" the Trojan [V. vii.5 ff.]. That isn't the plan Achilles has either
in the Troy Book or in the Recuyell. There, it is to slay Hector

when he is in an unfavorable position for his own defense. The deed Achilles performs himself.

Shakespeare was indebted to Caxton or to Lydgate for the idea of a plan: not the plan itself. That appears to be his own conception, though it is possible that he transferred to Hector's death the circum-stances under which Troilus meets his death as it occurs in the Troy Book and in the Recuyell. In Caxton's words, Achilles ordered his Myrmidons "to inclose Troylus" [Rec.II.638; AH, 550]. The re-semblance stops there, for though the Myrmidons unarm him, Achilles slays him.

It should be observed that in the Iron Age, the Myrmidons kill Hector, though Achilles strikes a blow after he is slain. He "fals slayne by the Mermidons, then Achilles wounds him with his Lance" [Dr.Wks. III.321]. Heywood's version is a combination of the accounts of Caxton or Lydgate, or both, and Shakespeare.

Shakespeare dramatized the incident of Hector's stripping a knight of armour, which both Lydgate and Caxton describe, when Hector meets his death. Hector's covetousness is mentioned by Homer but he is not robbing a corpse when he is slain. Heywood, as we have seen, omits this incident. The Myrmidons slay Hector when he is fully armed. He is overwhelmed by sheer numbers.

The last detail to be considered in Shakespeare's treatment of Hector's death, namely, Achilles' tying Hector's body to his horse's tail, is problematic, since Book XXII of the Iliad had not been trans-lated into English at this time. The particular situation is not in the Troy Book, nor in the Recuyell, though in these accounts Troilus is dragged by Achilles. Shakespeare could have made the transfer, since it appears he did transfer one detail from the account of Troilus' death to Hector's.

It is a probable assumption, though, that Shakespeare learned of this Homeric detail, not through the original, but through an indi-rect source, either from Virgil[1] or from Marlowe.[2] An Elizabethan who had done even a minimum of reading in the classics would be bound to know about the circumstances of Hector's death.[3]

The rough composition of the last scenes of the play led some scholars to assume that the conclusion of the fifth act, as it now stands, is not wholly Shakespeare's own work as he wrote it, but the product of multiple authorship.[4] Kittredge, however, saw no reason for the assumption. "The huddled appearance of the last

1. Troilus and Cressida, ed. W. J. Rolfe, p. 215, n. 22.
2. Dido, II.i.201 ff. in The Life of Marlowe and the Tragedy of Dido, ed. C. F. Tucker Brooke (London, 1903).
3. Interestingly enough this is the third situation in Book XXII that Shakespeare shows knowledge of. See above, pp. 52–53, p. 59. T. W. Baldwin points out a reference to an action that lies outside the translated books.—Shakespeare's Small Latine & Lesse Greeke (Urbana, 1944), II, 659.
4. Ibid., II, 659 ff.

six scenes need not shake one's faith. As presented on the curtain-
less Elizabethan stage these were merely the several events in
one continuous action with no shifting of scenery." [5]
    In writing the combat scenes, Shakespeare attempted to present
in dramatic form such hand-to-hand encounters as are described
so frequently in his sources. Often one man has many fights, and
often with the same person. Battle is joined, broken off (sometimes
by mutual consent, and sometimes by interference), and rejoined
later. Homer describes the nature of the combats which Shakespeare presented dramatically.

                        And as amids the skie
        We sometimes see an Omenous star blase cleare
            and dreadfully
        Then run his golden head in cloudes, and straight
            appeare againe
        So Hector otherwhiles did grace, the vantguarde
            shining plaine
        Then in the rereguarde hid himselfe, and laborde
            euerie where
        To order and encourage all . . . .

In this instance, Hector is described as performing the duties
of a leader. In actual combat, the same technique of appearing
here and there to deliver a stroke is characteristic of the type of
warfare Shakespeare portrayed in the last scenes of the play.

13. The Thersites Scenes

HOMER

    In the Iliades, Thersites, considering the little we hear about
him during the action of the war, would be called a minor character: yet considering the time he plays his part, and the opinions
he voices in council, he is, temporarily, of major importance. He
is the kind of person who makes himself heard in high places only
when unusual events take place in his presence, and some are
allowed a say who would never be heard in council. Thersites was
always a dissenter and opponent of the war, if we are to believe
Ulysses, and especially a critic of Agamemnon's policy. He does
not have opportunity to express his sentiments until after the
leaders and soldiers show manifest distaste for the war, and prepare to leave for Greece. Ulysses is able with divine aid to stop
that movement, but in council Thersites expresses a general
sentiment about the conduct of the war before Ulysses can re-es-
tablish Agamemnon's policy in good repute. Thersites' perspec-

5. G. L. Kittredge, Complete Works of Shakespeare (Ginn & Co.,
1936), p. 880.

tive is very different from that of the actual leaders of the expedition, but he voices the feelings of those who see the action from his own angle of vision.

To Ulysses, of course, Thersites is a prime example of insubordination, and the prompter of evil opinions throughout the host. But Thersites has eyes that see, and though Ulysses subdues him with blows, his criticism remains. Ulysses' oratory glosses over but does not answer his attack. Indeed, he attempts no real explanation; for the aristocratic ruler is not accountable to a rogue for his policy.

To complement his base mind, Homer gave Thersites an ill-formed body. His physical appearance is as ugly as his attitude.

> All sate, and sylent vsde their seates, Thersites
>   sole except,
> A man of tongue, whose rauenlike voice,[1] a tuneless
>   iarring kept,
> Who in his ranke minde coppy had of vnregarded
>   wordes,
> That rashly and beyond al rule, vsde to oppugne the
>   Lords,
> What whatsoeuer came from him, was laught at
>   mightilie:
> The filthiest Greeke that came to Troy: he had a
>   goggle eye,
> Starcke-lame he was of eyther foote: his shoulders
>   were contract,
> Into his brest and crookt withall: his head was sharpe
>   compact,
> And here and there it had a hayre . . . .[2]
>   [Iliades, pp. 26–27]

He holds Agamemnon and Ulysses culpable for the soldiers' mis-

1. Shakespeare seems to have remembered the adjective "rauenlike." His Thersites remarks "I would croak like a raven; I would bode, I would bode." (Troilus and Cressida, V. ii. 186–88.)

2. Iliades, pp. 26–27. Douglas Bush calls attention to early descriptions of Homer's Thersites, "Notes on Shakespeare's Classical Mythology," PQ, VI (1927), 298–99. "Homere in his Iliade describeth one Thersites / that he was most foule and euyll fauored of all the Grekes that came to the batayle of Troye / for he was both gogle eyed / and lame on the one legge / with croked and penched shulders and a long pyked hede / balde in very many places. And besyde these fautes he was a great folysshe babler / and ryght foule mouthed / and ful of debate and stryfe / carrynge alwayes agaynst the heddes and wyse men of the armye." Leonard Cox, The Arte or Crafte of Rhethoryke, ed. Frederic I. Carpenter (University English Studies; Chicago, 1899), V, 53.

fortunes, and the most greedy of gain fòr themselves. He retained
much anger for Achilles.[3]

> . . . to mighty Thetides
> And wise Vlisses he retaind, much anger and disease:
> For still he chid them eagerlie: and then against the
>   state,
> Of Agamemnon he would rayle: the Greekes in vehement
>   hate,
> And high disdaine conceipted him: yet he with violent
>   throate,
> Would needes vpbraide the General: and thus himselfe
>   forgot.
>   Atrides why complainst thou now? what dost thou
>   couet more?
> Thy thriftie tents are full of coine, and thou hast women
>   store,
> Faire and well fauorde, which we Greekes, at euery
>   towne we take,
> Resigne to thee: thinkst thou, thou wantst some treasure
>   thou mightst make,
> To bee deduc't thee out of Troy, by one that comes to
>   seeke,
> His sonne for ransome: who my selfe, or any other
>   Greeke,
> Should bring thee captiue? or a wench, fild with her sweets
>   of youth,
> Which thou maist loue and priuate keepe, for thy insaciate
>   tooth?
> But it becomes not kings to tempt by wicked president:
> Their subjects to dishonestie: O mindes most impotent,
> Not Achiues but Achian gyrles, come fall aborde and
>   home:
> Let him concoct his pray alone, alone Troy ouercome,
> To make him know if our free eares, his proud commandes
>   would heare.
> In any thing: or not disdaine his longer yoke to beare,[4]
> Who hath with contumely wrongd, a better man then hee . . . .
> . . . .
> Achilles hath no splene in him, but most remislie beares,
> A femall stomacke . . . .   [p. 27]

3. In the play, Thersites' most calumniating remarks are directed
against Achilles, Ulysses, and Agamemnon, as they were in the
Iliades. Shakespeare extended the sphere of Thersites' hate to include all members of the Greek expedition. It should be ·observed.
that in the epic, no one takes him seriously: ". . . whatsoeuer came
from him, was laught at mightilie"; "the Greekes in vehement hate,
And high disdaine conceipted him."
4. Shakespeare's Thersites speaks of the "yoke" to which Ajax and
Achilles are bound to plough up the wars. "There's Ulysses, and old

It is noticeable that Ulysses makes no attempt to answer Thersites' charges.

>   . . . prating Thersites cease,
> Though thou canst raile so cunninglie: nor dare to tempt
>   the peace,
> Of sacred kings, for well thou knowest, I know well what
>   thou art:
> A baser wretch came not to Troy to take the Grecians
>   part,
> Prophane not kings then with thy lips; examine our
>   retreate:
> Whereof our selues are ignorant, nor our states so
>   greate,
> That we dare vrge vpon the king, what he will onelie
>   know:
> Sit then and cease thy barbarous-tauntes to him whome
>   all we owe
> So much obseruance though from thee these insolent
>   poisons flow . . . .   [pp. 27-28]

Ulysses' reproof is not confined to words. He lays blows on Thersites' person, and drives him from the hall.[5]

> This said, his backe and shoulder blades he with his
>   scepter smit:
> Who then shrunke round and downe his cheekes the seruile
>   teares did flit:
> The golden scepter in his flesh a bloody print did raise,
> With which he trembling tooke his seat, and looking
>   twentie waies,
> Ill fauoredlie he wipte the teares from his selfe pittying
>   eyes . . . .   [p. 28]

Characteristically, the men who approved Thersites now howl at his exit, and take to heart Ulysses' plan for order and perseverance in the war.

> And then though all the host were sad they laught to heare
>   his cries,
> When thus flew speeches intermixt, O Gods what endles
>   good,
> Vlisses still bestowes on vs? that to the field of bloud,
> Instructs vs: and in counsaile doth, for chiefe director
>   serue,[6]
> Yet neuer action past his hands, that did more praise
>   deserue.

Nestor . . . yoke you like draught-oxen and make you plough up the wars." —Troilus and Cressida, II.i.113 ff.

5. In the play, it is Ajax who has the beating of Thersites.

6. Shakespeare's Ulysses is also chief in council.

>   Then to disgrace this rayling foole, in all the armies
>   .sight.
>   Whose rudenes henceforth will take heed: how he doth
>   princes bite.   [p. 28]

SHAKESPEARE

Achilles, Ajax, Patroclus, and other leaders who are hostile to
Agamemnon and his policy represent the top of the insubordinate
chain: Thersites is the bottom, but all are infected with the same
spirit of revolt against supreme authority which is delaying the
promised victory.

>   And in the imitation of these twain [Achilles,
>   Patroclus],
>   Who, as Ulysses says, opinion crowns
>   With an imperial voice, many are infect.
>   Ajax is grown self-will'd, and bears his head
>   In such a rein, in full as proud a place
>   As broad Achilles; keeps his tent like him;
>   Makes factious feasts; rails on our state of war,
>   Bold as an oracle, and sets Thersites,
>   A slave whose gall coins slanders like a mint,
>   To match us in comparisons with dirt;
>   To weaken and discredit our exposure,
>   How rank soever rounded in with danger. [I.iii.185-96]

In Troilus and Cressida, Thersites does not appear until Act II,
scene i. He is then in company with Ajax and, in spite of the latter's
interruptions, continues to vent his spleen on Agamemnon. His
complaint is that the leader of the army is not capable of producing
anything. Only if he had boils that "did run," " Then would come
some matter from him: I see none now" [II.i.9 ff.]. Ajax who can
gain his attention only by beating him, hears nothing complimentary.
Thersites ridicules Ajax's mental capacities, and charges him with
jealousy of Achilles.

>   Thou grumblest and railest every hour on Achilles, and
>   thou art as full of envy at his greatness as Cerberus is at
>   Proserpina's beauty, ay, that thou barkest at him. [II.i.34-37]

Achilles and Patroclus deliver Thersites from additional blows,
but that does not spare them Thersites' scorn.

>   . . . a great deal of your wit too lies in your sinews, or else
>   there be liars. Hector shall have a great catch if he knock
>   out either of your brains: a' were as good crack a fusty nut
>   with no kernel.   [II.i.107-11]

In coarse terms he shows both Achilles and Ajax their "true" position in the army. They are but slaves for hire.

>   There's Ulysses, and old Nestor, whose wit was mouldy
>   ere your grandsires had nails on their toes, yoke you like
>   draught-oxen and make you plough up the wars. [II.i.113-16]

In the last scene of the same act, Thersites enters alone, lost
in the labyrinth of his fury. He has his own way of saying what
Ulysses had said quite differently in council. "If Troy be not taken
till these two [Achilles, Ajax] undermine it, the walls will stand
till they fall of themselves" [II.iii.9-11]. Unlike Ulysses, he delves
into the causes of the war, and sees in the activity of the army only
a world of waste, and all for "a placket." He repudiates any feeling
of patriotism in so foolish a cause, and even wishes ill-luck attend
further ventures.

> After this, the vengeance on the whole camp! or rather,
> the Neapolitan bone-ache? for that, methinks, is the curse
> dependant on those that war for a placket. I have said my
> prayers, and, devil Envy, say Amen.   [II.iii.20-25]

In his brief colloquy with Achilles and Patroclus, Thersites
attempts to rouse them from their subservient position in the host.

> Agamemnon is a fool to offer to command Achilles; Achilles
> is a fool to be commanded of Agamemnon; Thersites is a fool
> to serve such a fool . . . .   [II.iii.68-71]

Since the cause is not worth the loss, the expedition deserves
whatever evil it provokes.

> Here is such patchery, such juggling, and such knavery! all
> the argument is a whore and a cuckhold; a good quarrel to
> draw emulous factions and bleed to death upon. Now, the dry
> serpigo on the subject! and war and lechery confound all!
>   [II.iii.77-82]

In Act III, scene iii, Thersites describes the effect on Ajax's
pride of his appointment to match arms with Hector. Thersites,
in this brief scene, is more comical than critical, though he gives
the departing Achilles an uncomplimentary jibe [II.iii.317ff.].

In Act V, scene i, Thersites is the bearer of Hecuba's letter to
Achilles. While the Myrmidon leader reads, Thersites defames
Patroclus' character, but he escapes without blows. When alone,
he discredits the reputations of Agamemnon and Menelaus. ". . . but
to be Menelaus! I would conspire against destiny" [V.i.70ff.].

Thersites next turns up spying abuses outside Diomedes' tent.
He finds evidence there of the lechery he had noted a common
element in the war.

> Would I could meet that rogue Diomed! I would croak like
> a raven; I would bode, I would bode. Patroclus will give me
> any thing for the intelligence of this whore: the parrot will
> not do more for an almond than he for a commodious drab.
> Lechery, lechery; still, wars and lechery: nothing else holds
> fashion. A burning devil take them!   [V.ii.186-93]

When Thersites is on the battle-ground alone, he again summa-
rizes the war as he sees it.

Now they are clapper-clawing one another; I'll go look on.
That dissembling abominable varlet, Diomed, has got that
same scurvy doting foolish young knave's sleeve of Troy
there in his helm: I would fain see them meet . . . . O' the
t'other side, the policy of those crafty-swearing rascals,
that stale old mouse-eaten dry cheese, Nestor, and that same
dog-fox, Ulysses, is not proved worth a blackberry: they set
me up, in policy, that mongrel cur, Ajax, against that dog of
as bad a kind, Achilles; and now is the cur Ajax prouder than
the cur Achilles, and will not arm to-day; whére upon the
Grecians begin to proclaim barbarism, and policy grows into
an ill opinion.   [V. iv. 1-20]

In his last appearances Thersites is a coward, but quick-witted
enough to escape the fate of a coward on the field [V. vii. 13 ff.].

HEYWOOD

In the Iron Age, Thersites makes his first appearance in a noble
gathering. "Enter King Menelaus, King Diomed, Thersites, a Lord
Embassadour with Attendants" [Dr. Wks. III. 273]. He is, apparently,
fit to associate with the kings and administrators of Greece. To his
counsel, Menelaus lends an open ear. In his first speech, he warns
Sparta's king against taking under his jurisdiction more lands, lest
he lose what he possesses, and maybe Helen to boot. Diomedes calls
him a "rayler," though Thersites quickly corrects that misrepre-
sentation, in words at least. "No, I disclaim't, I am a Counsellor"
[III. 274]. For a counselor, however, he assumes a manner of
speech quite dissimilar to that of his associates, and allows himself the privilege of making free observations that are not only
coarse but also rather impolitic. His many comments on the actions
and conversation of the main characters, which are usually brief
asides, are occasionally witty, frequently impertinent, and generally
tedious.

Heywood's Thersites doesn't wholly lack discernment, however.
He is the only member of the Spartan court who spies, in Paris'
visit, an evil motive.

> Men.   Thersites your opinion.
> Did'st euer see wisdome thus attir'd?
> Ther. I haue knowne villany hath lookt as
>   smooth
> As yon briske fellow.
> Men.   I am a foole then say.
> Ther. And so thou art,
> To hugge the Serpent fraud so neere your
>   heart.
> Men.   Shallow Thersites, my faire Prince
>   of Troy
> Welcome, come sit betwixt my Queene and
>   mee.

> Ther. Hee'le one day stand betwixt thy Queene
> and thee.
> I haue obseru'd, 'tis still the Cuckholds fate
> To hugge that knaue who helps to horne his
> pate.   [Dr.Wks.III.280-81]

After Menelaus discovers the truth of this saw, and has, with the aid of Greece, raised the siege of Troy, Thersites comments on the nature of the undertaking.

> Braue time, rare change, from fighting now to
> feasting:
> So many heauy blades to flye in peeces
> For such a peece of light flesh? what's the reason?
> A Lasse of my complexion, and this feature
> Might haue bin rapt, and stolne agayne by Paris,
> And none of all this stirre for't: but I perceiue
> Now all the World's turn'd wenchers, and in time
> All wenches will turne witches . . . .   [III.301-2]

To avail himself of what the world now offers, he contemplates a disguise to hide his "hutch-backe," and plans to deck himself in the clothes of a courtier to better accomplish his amorous inclinations. Rather quickly, however, he decides against camouflage, and will appear to others in his own "humour," which is to "brauely rayle" [III.302].

When Thersites, by his boldness, provokes an argument with Achilles, he recalls Shakespeare's character. He tries to reveal how the actions of Achilles appear to the Grecian host.

> Where's this great sword and buckler man of Greece?
> Wee shall haue him one of sneakes noise,
> And come peaking into the Tents of the Greeks,
> With will you haue any musicke Gentlemen.
> . . . .
> . . . hee's [Hector] in the field, thou in thy Tent,
> Hector playing vpon the Greekish burgonets,
> Achilles fingring his effeminate Lute.
> And now because thou durst not meete him in the field, thou
> hast counterfeited an honour of loue. Achilles? Thou the
> Champion of Greece, a meere bug-beare, a scar-crow, a
> Hobby-horse.   [III.312]

In his conversation with Troilus on the battle-field, he ridicules the cause of the war.

> I came to laugh at mad-men, thou art one;
> The Troians are all mad, so are the Greeks,
> To kill so many thousands for one drabbe,
> For Hellen: a light thing, doe thou turne wise
> And kill no more; I since these warres began
> Shed not one drop of blood.   [III.325]

Thersites is a coward on the field, but he has no fear of Achilles'
wrath, which he always provokes.

> Ther. Thou art a coward.
> Achil. Haue I not sau'd thy life, and slaine
> proud Troilus
> By whom the Greekes lye pilde in breathlesse heapes?
> Ther. Yes when he was out of breath so thou slewest
> Hector
> Girt with thy Mirmidons.
> Achil. Dogged Thersites,
> I'll cleaue thee to thy Nauell if thou op'st
> Thy venemous Iawes.
> Ther. Doe, doe, good Dog-killer.
> Achil. You slaue.   [III.327]

Thersites, after he has given directions to the soldiers for the
proper arrangement of the seats for the judges of the Ajax-Ulysses
debate, passes brief judgment on the natures of the contestants:

> . . . where's the Armour,
> The prize for which the crafty Fox Vlisses,
> And mad Bull Aiax, must this day contend?   [III.334]

A fuller picture of the qualities of the leaders of Troy Thersites
offers to Ajax after the contest. He begins on Ajax.

> Who thou the son of Telamon, thou art a foole, an Asse,
> a very blocke. What makest thou here at Troy to ayde a
> Cuckold, beeing a Bachelour? Paris hath stolne no wife of
> thine: if Aiax had beene ought but the worst of these, he
> might haue kept his Country, solac'd his father, and com-
> forted his mother: what thankes hast thou for spending thy
> meanes, hazarding thy souldiers? wasting thy youth, loosing
> thy blood, indangering thy life?
> . . . what thankes hast thou for all thy trauaile? Vlisses
> hath the armour, and what art thou now reckoned? a good
> moyle, a horse that knowes not his owne strength, an Asse
> fit for service, and good for burthens, to carry gold, and
> to feede on thistles . . . .   [III.342]

His comments on the other leaders of Troy are as would be expected: Agamemnon, "A blind Iustice and I would he had kist Fortunes blind cheekes, when hee could not see to doe thee Iustice";
Menelaus, "A King and a Cuckold, and a horne-plague consume
him"; Diomed, "A very bench-whistler; and loues Cresida Hell
and confusion swallow him"; Ulysses, "A dam'd politician, Scilla
and Charibdis swallow him"; and of himself, "A Rogue, a rayling
Rogue, a Curr, a barking Dog, the Pox take mee else" [III.343].[7]

---

7. In spite of such talk about the Greek leaders, the charge of an
anti-Homeric, anti-idealistic attitude towards the Greek heroes

In part II of the Iron Age, Thersites is still an actor, of a kind, but his appearances are less frequent. His closest associate is Synon. His counsel is still prized by Menelaus, who on his urgent advice, primarily, takes Helen back as his wife.

> Thy browes beare hornes already, but who sees them?
> When thou return'st to Sparta, some will thinke
> Thou art a Cuckold, but who is't dare say so?
> Thou art a King, thy sinnes are clouded o're,
> Where poore mens faults by tongues are made much more.
> Of all men liuing, Kings are last shall heare
> Of their dishonours . . . .   [III. 388]

Thersites meets a violent death in the general fight that develops when Orestes attacks Pyrrhus [III.427].

Since Shakespeare created him, Thersites has been taken for about everything but what he represents in the play. For a character, he has had many likenesses, none of which has fitted him sufficiently well to satisfy the succeeding critic of the veracity of the portrait. He has been many persons, and many symbols since his conception. He has been a fool, a chorus, Shakespeare's voice speaking against classical form and character which Chapman attempted to popularize, Thomas Dekker, or the expression of Shakespeare's pessimism which the dramatist supposedly endured at one period in his life, and which prevented him from seeing nobility in men's actions. To Spencer he is a "corrosive" railer; to O. J. Campbell, "a railer, a detractor, and a buffoon," the elaboration of whose character was owing to the dramatist's attempt to transform Homer's Thersites "into one of the conventional, well-nigh indispensable characters of the new satiric comedy." [8]
In addition to what he has been in the history of criticism, Thersites has consistently brought down on his head unrelieved contempt. No other character that Shakespeare brought to life has been more abused by the commentators. The world is as hard on

has not been brought against Heywood's portrayal of classical history: yet it might as reasonably be as it has been brought against Shakespeare's.
8. W. W. Lawrence, Shakespeare's Problem Comedies, p. 141; J. Foster Palmer, "On Certain Phases in the Evolution of Ethics," Transactions of the Royal Society of Literature, 2nd ser., XV (1893), 69; Arthur Acheson, Shakespeare and the Rival Poet (London & New York, 1903), pp. 200 ff.; Frederick G. Fleay, A Chronicle History of the Life and Work of William Shakespeare (London, 1886), p. 221; George Brandes, William Shakespeare (London, 1920), pp. 501 ff.; Theodore Spencer, Shakespeare and the Nature of Man (New York, 1942), p. 114; Oscar J. Campbell, Shakespeare's Satire (Oxford, 1943), pp. 106–7.

Thersites as he was on his own world. It is, however, permissible
to think that the critics, in giving so much attention to Thersites,
have overemphasized his importance in the drama. His dramatic
value is limited. It is his volubility that makes him seem more
important than he is. The main trouble with Thersites is that he
is too "good" a character. He has more vitality than many of the
major characters. And his remarks, most of which have some
truth in them, leave an impression which cynical and salacious
observations are wont to do.

Critics think that Shakespeare degraded Ajax, Patroclus, and
Achilles, by allowing those heroes to banter with such a knave.
But in the contact the leaders have with the rogue is an illustration
of Ulysses' description of the breakdown of the order of the army.
The insubordinate members tend to gather.

Furthermore, in Thersites' absolute disdain for all superiors
(he is the man of lowest degree), is the lively exhibition of that
disease Ulysses had commented on:

> The general's disdain'd
> By him one step below, he by the next,
> That next by him beneath; so every step,
> Exampled by the first pace that is sick
> Of his superior, grows to an envious fever
> Of pale and bloodless emulation.   [I.iii.129-34]

Throughout he matches, as Ulysses notes, the great leaders " in
comparisons with dirt, To weaken and discredit" them.

Sometimes Thersites sees the truth: ". . . too much blood, and
too little brain," he says, characterizing Achilles and Patroclus.
But more often he sees only part of the truth. He sees the war
simply as a war for a "placket," and from a certain point of view,
he is right. The flaws he notes in each of the Greek leaders are
there. Ulysses and Nestor do yoke Ajax and Achilles like oxen,
and force them to plough up the wars, yet he has no conception of
the feelings of Ajax and Achilles, who have been trained to seek
glory and honor in wielding and matching arms.

Thersites is an admirable portrait of that common kind of person
who cannot see beyond the worst in a present situation, but using
that as a foundation, builds up a picture of an event or of a character which is really distorted, though partially correct. Shakespeare
has portrayed in him the Malcontent in War, but a Malcontent of
low degree.

In most respects, Shakespeare's Thersites is closer to Homer's
than to Heywood's. But essentially, all three characters are similar.
In the epic, Thersites has no social position, or that is the impression one gains from Ulysses' words [Iliades, p. 26]. In Troilus
and Cressida, his standing is certainly no better, possibly worse,
for he is not allowed a voice in council. Nestor calls him "a slave,"
and he appears to be Ajax's fool. In the play, Ulysses remarks to
Nestor, "Achilles hath inveigled his [Ajax's] fool from him" [II.

iii.98]. And Achilles once speaks of him as if he were an allowed
fool [II.iii.63]. In the Iron Age, however, Thersites appears to
occupy a lofty position.[9] He is frequently in the company of the
leaders of the expedition, and is a counselor Menelaus heeds.
Railing is his method of imparting advice, but he occupies a re-
spectable position, which his namesake does not, either in the epic
or in Shakespeare's play. He is, however, at least once called "a
slave" by Achilles, yet the expression is used in an argument.

Homer describes his physical deformities in detail: in Troilus
and Cressida, Ajax says he will beat him into handsomeness [II.
ii.16]. In the Iron Age, he is "a hutch-backe" [Dr.Wks.III.302]; in
the Iliades, "his shoulders were contract" [Iliades, p. 27].

Homer's Thersites does not express himself in the colloquial
or vulgar style employed by Shakespeare's and Heywood's Thersiteses
to make their points.There is in the dramatists' conception of his
language a similiarity, and on occasions, a likeness of expression.
"When rank Thersites opes his mastic jaws" [I.iii.73] may have
stuck in Heywood's mind and passed into Achilles' description of
his tormentor: "I'll cleaue thee to thy Nauell if thou op'st Thy
venemous Iawes" [Dr.Wks.III.327]. Shakespeare's character calls
Ulysses a "dog-fox" [V.iv.13]; Heywood's Thersites also likens
Ulysses to a "Fox" [III.334], although Ulysses' craft was, of course,
traditional, and the association of the fox with craft likewise traditional. If there is a debt in certain details of one dramatist to
the other, Heywood was more than likely indebted to Shakespeare.

In all accounts, Thersites is mindful of the lechery in the armies.
In the Iliades, the greater part of his speech in council is a diatribe
against Agamemnon's lustfulness. Shakespeare, in developing Thersites' character for his play, had ample warrant to make him a
constant critic of lechery. Thersites, in the epic, principally accuses
Agamemnon of this vice: the other leaders by implication.[10]

> Atrides why complainst thou now? what dost thou
>   couet more?
> Thy thriftie tents are full of coine, and thou hast
>   women store,
> Faire and well fauorde, which we Greekes, at euery
>   towne we take,
> Resigne to thee: thinkst thou, thou wantst some treasure
>   thou mightst make,
> To bee deduc't thee out of Troy, by one that comes
>   to seeke,
> His sonne for ransome: who my selfe, or any other
>   Greeke,   [Iliades, p. 27] .

9. Tatlock, PMLA, XXX (1915), 723, n. 60.
10. Shakespeare's Thersites' observation of "wars and lechery" is
the Homeric character's argument in brief.

> Should bring thee captiue? or a wench, fild with her
>   sweetes of youth,
> Which thou maist loue and priuate keepe for thy
>   insaciate tooth?   [p. 27]

In the Iron Age, Thersites notes the lustfulness of the Greeks [Dr. Wks. III.334], but by no means places the stress on it Shakespeare's Thersites does.

Shakespeare developed his characterization of Thersites (as Dr. Johnson long ago noted), from Homer's description of the man. The dramatist has not changed his nature in any marked degree. He has increased the number of people Thersites hates, given him a language more fitting the camp and his rank than the council, and enlarged upon his cynical outlook. Above all, Shakespeare built up his character to represent in the lower ranks of the command, a living exemplum of a Malcontent who is most voluble in expressing his disdain for his many superiors. He should be seen within the context of Ulysses' description of the behaviour and attitude of the Greeks during the stalemate.

Doubtless Shakespeare's contemporaries finally regarded Thersites much as did Ben Jonson: "Homer's Thersites . . . speaking without judgement, or measure." [11]

14. The Trojan Council

SHAKESPEARE

In Troilus and Cressida, Shakespeare dramatized two council scenes. In the first, Agamemnon summons the Greek leaders to call their attention to the serious condition of the army. Ulysses diagnoses the cause of the weakness in the command and later, in the same scene, proposes a cure. The statement of the present condition is the dramatic exposition: the proposed cure, the indication of the beginning of the dramatic action, or the plot.

In the second council scene, Priam is in conference with his councilors, who comprise his family, to decide on present policy and action. What they considered a wise and just deed in the past (the seizure of Helen for Hesione), now appears to have been an unwise act. Whether to follow the law of nature, and send Helen back to her husband, or to keep her and to suffer the consequences that infringement of that law will exact, is an issue which faces Priam. It demands instant decision, since Nestor has sent a proposal to the Trojans:

> " Deliver Helen, and all damage else,
>   As honour, loss of time, travail, expense,

11. Ben Jonson, Discoveries, ed. Herford and Simpson (London, 1947), VIII, 574.

> Wounds, friends, and what else dear that is
>   consum'd
> In hot digestion of this comorant war,
> Shall be struck off."   [II.ii.3-7]

Hector, Priam's eldest son, and leader of the Trojan armies,
shows himself cautious in council. He has no personal fear of
what may follow disregard of the Greek note, but on the other
hand, he does not overlook general evil consequences, beyond
his personal endeavors to mitigate, that eventually may result.
"Who knows what follows?" Helen, who is not Trojan in the first
place, is not worth the loss of life involved in keeping her.

>   Let Helen go:
> Since the first sword was drawn about this
>   question,
> Every tithe soul, 'mongst many thousand dismes,
> Hath been as dear as Helen; I mean, of ours:
> If we have lost so many tenths of ours,
> To guard a thing not ours nor worth to us,
> Had it our name, the value of one ten,
> What merit's in that reason which denies
> The yielding of her up?   [II.ii.17-25]

Troilus is outraged to think that Hector would even consider
measuring in common terms the value of one the king has placed
his approval on [II.ii.25-27].
Helenus, of course, as seer and prophet, supports Hector

>   Should not our father
> Bear the great sway of his affairs with reasons,
> Because your speech hath none that tells him so?
>   [II.ii.34-36]

Troilus has no understanding of, or at least sympathy for, the
views Helenus expresses. To fur one's gloves with reason in war
is folly, and the quick road to inertia.

>   Nay, if we talk of reason,
> Let's shut our gates and sleep: manhood and honour
> Should have harehearts, would they but fat their
>   thoughts
> With this cramm'd reason: reason and respect
> Make livers pale and lustihood deject.   [II.ii.46-50]

Hector shows no inclination to enter into abstruse argument.
He returns to his former assertion. Helen is not worth the cost.

>   'Tis mad idolatry
> To make the service greater than the god:
> And the will dotes that is inclinable
> To what infectiously itself affects,
> Without some image of the affected merit. [II.ii.56-60]

Troilus, in his reply, reviews the past policy of the state, and well points out that at one time, at least, the service was held no greater than the god, and that the council's decision was deemed worthy of consent.
                                        It was thought meet
        Paris should do some vengeance on the Greeks:
        Your breath of full consent bellied his sails;
        The seas and winds, old wranglers, took a truce
        And did him service: he touch'd the ports desir'd,
        And for an old aunt whom the Greeks held captive,
        He brought a Grecian queen . . . .
        . . . .
        If you'll avouch 'twas wisdom Paris went,
        As you must needs, for you all cried "Go, go" ;
        If you'll confess he brought home noble prize,
        As you must needs, for you all clapp'd your hands,
        And cried "Inestimable!'' why do you now
        The issue of your proper wisdoms rate,
        And do a deed that Fortune never did,
        Beggar the estimation which you prized
        Richer than sea and land?   [II.ii.72-92]

To return Helen now, after the state approved the action that brought her to Troy, is to turn "back upon the merchant" the silks, "When we have soil'd them"—a deed consonant neither with past policy, nor with present honorable behaviour.
    Cassandra replies to Troilus, though to him, her ideas are mad.
                            . . . her brain-sick raptures
        Cannot distaste the goodness of a quarrel
        Which hath our several honours all engag'd
        To make it gracious.   [II.ii.122-25]

    Paris, of course, sees no advantage to be gained in releasing Helen.
        Well may we fight for her whom, we know well,
        The world's large spaces cannot parallel.[II.ii.161-62]

Hector, after he has heard the opinions Paris and Troilus express, and the fearful prophecy of Cassandra, guides the argument back to more normal channels. The moral issue, which his brothers have overlooked, is the only issue on which decision to yield Helen, or to keep her, should be made. The law of nature demands, without question, that she be returned to Menelaus.
                            Nature craves
        All dues be render'd to their owners: now,
        What nearer debt in all humanity
        Than wife is to the husband? If this law
        Of nature be corrupted through affection,
        And that great minds, of partial indulgence
        To their benumbed wills, resist the same,
        There is a law in each well-order'd nation
        To curb those raging appetites that are
        Most disobedient and refractory.   [II.ii.173-82]

Hector knows what should be done, and says in no uncertain terms what should be done. But he also knows what the voice of the council is, and, of course, he has a predilection for that glory and renown that Troilus and even Paris hope to win in combat. In addition, the policy that Priam decided long ago cannot be replaced at this late date, and on the instant with another, without giving an opportunity to the world at large to accuse the Trojans of levity in council and in their undertakings.

> My spritely brethren, I propend to you
> In resolution to keep Helen still;
> For 'tis a cause that hath no mean
>   dependance
> Upon our joint and several dignities.   [II.ii.190-93]

Hector concurs in Troilus' rapturous appraisal of what Helen is, what honor is.

> But, worthy Hector,
> She is a theme of honour and renown,
> A spur to valiant and magnanimous deeds,
> Whose present courage may beat down our foes,
> And fame in time to come canonise us;
> For, I presume, brave Hector would not lose
> So rich advantage of a promis'd glory
> As smiles upon the forehead of this action
> For the wide world's revenue.   [II.ii.198-206]

CAXTON

The meeting of the Trojan leaders in the Recuyell which is comparable to the scene in Troilus and Cressida in length and in general substance, takes place before the fighting in the Ten Years' War begins. Priam summons his council and the influential citizens of Troy, to explain to them his desire to compensate Troy for the loss of Hesione by some act of revenge on the Greeks, and he wishes to hear the expression of the people, whether they will support or disapprove such an action.

> . . . and after hee assembled on a day all his noble men in his pallace of Ilion, and saide vnto them. Ye know how by your councell, Anthenor was sent into Greece for to recouer my sister Exione, & that by fair meanes. Ye too verie well know also, howe that hee is returned and come backe, and also what wronges and opprobries he hath found. And me seemeth that the Greeks make little account of the iniuries that they haue done vnto vs, at the least, they by their wordes repent them not, but yet they menace vs more strongly then euer they did. God forbid that euer it shoulde come vnto vs, like as they menace vs. But I pray the gods to giue vs power to auenge vs to their losse . . . If ye thinke it good, we will send our men secretly, that shall do to them great dammage, ere that they shall be readie for to defend themselues.   [Rec.II.516-17; AH, 444-45]

All those present advise the king of their full consent to his
decision. After the nobles clear the hall, Priam speaks to his
inner council, where policy is made and executed.

> My sonnes, ye haue well in your memorie the death of
> your Grandfather, the seruitude of your Aunt Exione, that
> they holde by your life in manner of a common woman. And
> you be so puissant, me seemeth that reason should instruct
> you, for to employ your selfe to reuenge this great iniurie
> and shame. And if this mooue you not thereto, yet yee ought
> to doe it to satisfie my will and pleasure: for I am ready to
> die for sorrow and anguish, which ye ought & and be bound
> for to remedie to your power . . . . And thou Hector . . . I
> pray thee first, that thou enterprise to put in execution this
> my will.   [Rec.II.517–18; AH, 445–46]

Hector reveals himself to be an expedient councilor, even as
does Shakespeare's Hector in council. No one is more sensitive
to wrong, no one keener to avenge it. But, on the other hand, not
to weigh the consequence that the revenge will provoke, is to
hazard a course whose end is doubtful, and which reason cannot
approve.

> . . . there is none of all your sonnes, but that it seemeth to
> him a thing humane, to desire vengeaunce of these iniuries,
> and to vs that be of high noblenesse, a little iniurie ought to
> be great. As it is so that the qualitie of the person groweth
> and diminisheth, so ought the qualitie of the iniurie. And if
> wee be desirous and haue appetite to take vengeance of our
> iniuries, we forsake not, nor leaue the nature of men: for in
> like manner doe and vse the dumbe beastes to doo, and nature
> it selfe teacheth and guideth them thereto. My right deere
> Lord and father, there is none of all your sonnes that ought
> more to desire the vengeaunce of the iniurie and death of
> our Lord and grandfather, then I that am the eldest. But I
> will (if it please you) that yee consider in this enterprise,
> not only the beginning, but also the middle and the end, to
> what perill wee may come heereafter, for otherwhile little
> profite some things well begunne that come to an euill end.
> Then me thinketh, that it is much more allowable for a
> man to absteine him for to beginne thinges whereof the endes
> bee dangerous, and whereof may come more euill then good:
> for any thing is not said to be fortunate or happie vntill the
> time that it come vnto a good end. I say not these thinges
> for anie euill meaning or cowardise: but only to the end that
> ye beginne not a thing, and specially that thing that yee haue
> in your heart to put in practise but that ye first be well
> counselled.   [Rec.II.518–19; AH, 446–47]

Hector reminds Priam how strong are the Greeks that have as
subject all "Affricke and Europe": how many powerful knights they
can assemble for an army. Hesione is not worth the cost of the
venture. Besides, she is old.

Exione is not of so high prise, that it behooueth all vs to
put vs in perill and danger of death for her. [It is better for
her to remain in Greece] . . . then we shoulde put vs all in
such perils. And meekly I beseech you, not to suppose in
any wise, that I say these things for cowardise: But I doubt
the chaunces of fortune, and least that vnder the shadows
of this thing she confound and destroie your great seignorie,
and least that wee should beginne thinges that we ought to
leaue, for to eschew more great mischiefe . . . .
                                    [Rec.II.519–20; AH, 447]

Paris is not content with Hector's reasoning. He suggests that
Priam send him to Greece, and by so doing, exact vengeance on
the Greeks for the loss of his aunt, and also thereby fulfill the
prophecy in the dream he had while sleeping in the forest.

Deiphobus supports Paris' appeal, and begs Priam not to listen
to cautious reason.

My right deare Lord, if in all the works that men should
beginne, they should be aduised euer in the particularities
and singular things that might happen or fal, they should
neuer enterprise nor do valiant act by hardinesse. If the
labourers should leaue to care and sowe the land, for the
seed that the birdes picke vp and gather, they should neuer
labour. And therefore (right deare father) let vs make ready
for to send into Greece of your shippes
                              [Rec.II.522–23; AH, 449–50]

Helenus replies to Deiphobus in Cassandra's vein.

Beware that couetousnesse of vengeance put not in you
such danger as lieth herein. Ye know very well, howe I
vnderstand and can the science to knowe the things future
and to come, as yee haue proued many times without finding
fault: the gods forbidde, that it euer come that Paris be sent
into Greece. For know ye for certaine, that if he goe to make
any assault, ye shall see this noble and honourable citie
destroyed . . . .   [Rec.II.523; AH, 450]

The council is perturbed by Helenus' prophecy. Troilus, however,
rises from his place, and discredits the observations his brother
made.

. . . O noble men and hardy, how be ye abashed for the wordes
of this coward priest here? Is it not the custome of Priestes
for to dread the battailes by pusillanimitie, and for to loue
good cheere and pleasures, & to fill their bellies with good
wines and with good meats? Who is he that beleeueth that any
man may know the things to come, vnlesse the gods do shew
it him by reuelation? It is but follie for to tarie vpon this, or
to beleeue such things. If Helenus be afrayd, let him go into
the Temple, and sing the diuine Seruice, and let the other take
reuenge of their iniuries by strength and force of armes.
                                    [Rec.II.524; AH, 453]

Those that hear Troilus speak are impressed by his words, and
Priam is given general support in the undertaking he proposed.
When Cassandra learns the decision taken by the council, she fore-
tells the doom of Troy, but no admonitions can deter Priam from
what he wills. "But neither for the disswasions of Hector, neither
admonition nor warning of Cassandra, the king woulde not change
his purpose, nor for Helenus his son . . ." [Rec.II.527; AH, 453].

The proposal that Nestor sends to Priam in Troilus and Cressida
has for its closest counterpart in the Recuyell the message that
Diomede and Ulysses bear to Ilium before the opening of the war
against Troy. Agamemnon sends this embassy to Priam to request
the return of Helen, and to ask restitution of the damage Priam
did, when at the court of Menelaus. On their part, if Priam grants
the request, the Greeks will immediately return to their homeland,
satisfied in honor.

> . . . that we might returne into our countrey, without
> suffering of more paine, with our honour and worshippe,
> wee will send vnto the king Priamus our speciall messengers,
> and bidde him to send and deliuer againe to vs Helene freely,
> and that he restore vnto vs the dammages that Paris hath
> done in the Ile of Cythare: for if he will so do, our returne
> shalbe honourable . . . .   [Rec.II.558; AH, 481]

No council is summoned to act on the request of this embassy.
To the Trojans it is too obvious an affront to need deliberation and
discussion.

During the siege, however, Priam summons his council to determine whether or not to grant the Greek request for a truce.
Hector opposes granting the Greeks this favor, for under cover
of a truce, they will supply and revictual their army, which, if
unsupplied, might succumb to the pressure the Trojans can maintain [Rec.II.601; AH, 518]. But Hector's advice is not heeded, and
the truce is granted. Hector, though he has pronounced the truth,
bows to the general voice of the council. ". . . howbeit he woulde
not abide only by his intent against the opiniõ of so many wise men,
but agreed with the other . . ." [Rec.II.601; AH, 518].

HOMER

The first Trojan council described by Homer also gave Shakespeare a hint of the kind of policy formulated in Troy. Priam is apt
to take advice that is of no benefit to his country. When he should
be preparing for war, his thoughts are on peaceful measures. Iris
speaks to that effect to the assembled peers, in the voice of Polites.

> O Priam thou art alwaies pleasde, with indiscrete
>   aduice:
> And framest thy life to times of peace when such
>   a war doth rise
> As threates ineuitable spoile . . . .
>   [Iliades, p. 43/34 (in 1598 edition)]

The order Iris takes to Hector is for him to divide his forces,
so that some will protect the city, and others will engage the
enemy on the plain, in order that the Trojans may confront the
Greeks at whatever point they launch their attack.

> I neuer did behold:
> Such and so mightie troupes of men, who trample
>   on the mold,
> In number like <u>Autumnus</u> leaues, or like the maryne
>   sand;
> All ready round about the walles to vse their running
>   hand:
> Hector, I therefore charge thee most, this charge to
>   vndertake,
> A multitude remaine in Troy, will fight for Priams
>   sake;
> Of other lands and languages; let euery leader then:
> Bring forth well armd into the field his seuerall
>   bands of men.   [p. 43]

The second Trojan council is summoned after Hector returns
from the combat with Ajax, to pass on a resolution proposed by
Antenor that Helen be returned to Greece. To keep her is 'to defend
broken faiths. No good event can come to the offender.' It is better
for Troy to lose what it got wrongfully, and to survive, rather than
to retain the unlawful prize and perish as a consequence.

> . . . giue good eare to what my care commends:
> To your consents, for all our good: resolue, let vs
>   restore
> The Argiue Helen, with her wealth to him she had
>   before:
> We now defend but broken faiths: if therefore ye
>   refuse
> No good euent can I expect, of all the warres we
>   vse.   [p. 55]

Paris cannot believe Antenor is sane. He is content, however,
to return Helen's wealth, if that surrender will appease the Greeks.

> Antenor to myne eares thy words harsh and vngracious
>   bene:
> Thou canst vse better, if thou wilt, but if these truly
>   fit
> Thy serious thoughts, the Gods with age, have reft thy
>   healthfull wit:
> To warrelike Troians I will speake, I clearely doe deny,
> To yield my wife: but all her wealth I render willingly:
> What euer I from Argos brought, adioning to it more,
>   . . . if peace I may restore. [p. 55]

Priam dismisses the council and sends to Agamemnon the Trojan proposal. Diomedes quashes the plan by observing that so late
a proposal can only mean that Troy is about to fall. The Greek
leaders agree [pp. 56–57].

HEYWOOD

The meeting of the Trojan council that is dramatized in the <u>Iron Age</u> takes place before the Ten Years' War begins. Priam summons his council to inform them that he desires to redeem Hesione from her present slavery in Greece. Aeneas outlines to the councilors how strong new Troy is, and how many valiant sons and warlike supporters Priam has to make an aggressive policy a success. Hector, however, opposes any Trojan act that will reopen hostilities with the Greeks.

> In mine opinion we haue no iust cause
> To rayse new tumults, that may liue in peace:
> Warre is a fury quickly coniured vp,
> But not so soone appeased.   [Dr.Wks.III.266]

Both Troilus and Paris consider the reputation Troy has in the world, and to them, it does not appear to be a good one. Troy was destroyed twice by the Greeks in the past. Hesione is still a captive. Hector, on the other hand, thinks Troy was justly destroyed. As for Hesione, she belonged to Hercules.

> Fetch her that list: my reuerent King and father,
> If you pursue this expedition,
> By the vntaunted honor of these armes
> That liue imblazon'd on my burnish't shield,
> It is without good cause, and I deuine
> Of all your flourishing line, by which the Gods
> Haue rectified your fame aboue all Kings,
> Not one shall liue to meate your Sepulchre,
> Or trace your funerall Heralds to the Tombes
> Of your great Ancestours: oh for your honour
> Take not vp uniust Armes.   [III.267]

When Hector learns from Antenor, who returns from Greece during the council meeting, that Hesione is not held in the esteem her position demands, and that Priam's embassy was received by the Greeks without proper ceremony and respect, he suddenly abandons his former opposition to stirring up future strife, and vigorously supports a policy of aggression.

> By <u>Ioue</u> wee'le fetch her [Hesione] thence
> Or <u>make</u> all populous Greece a Wildernesse,
> <u>Paris</u> a hand, wee are <u>friends</u>, now <u>Greece</u> shall
>   finde
> And thou shalt know what mighty <u>Hector</u> dares.
> When all th'vnited Kings in <u>Armes</u> shall rue
> This base dishonour done to <u>Priams</u> blood.   [III.268]

Paris then proposes that he go into Greece and steal the fairest of Grecian queens. Cassandra, however, tries to block this action. Hector lends to her an half-willing ear, and loses something of the ardor Antenor's words inspired in him.

> Cassandra is a Vestall Prophetesse,
> And consecrate to Pallas; of inspir'd
> Then lende her gracious audience.   [III.270]

Hector says nothing further in this scene. When Helen arrives
with Paris, he informs her of his opposition to the plan that brought
her to Troy. Henceforth, however, he will be her champion.

> I was not forward to haue Paris sent,
> But being return'd th'art welcome: I desired not
> To haue bright Hellen brought, but being landed,
> Hector proclaimes himselfe her Champion
> 'Gainst all the world, and shall guard thee safe
> Despight all opposition.   [III.289]

The scene in Troilus and Cressida, in which the Trojan councilors debate the advantages or disadvantages of accepting or reject-
ing Nestor's proposal, has in certain details, and also in several
general aspects, resemblances to the scenes described by Shakespeare's predecessors: but for the most part, he so altered the
details that were suggestive to him, that it is not easy to follow him.

The council scene in the Troy Book (see Appendix I, x), the Recuyell,
and the Iron Age, takes place before the Ten Years' War. The action
decided on in council provokes the war. Subsequent meetings of the
council, according to Lydgate and Caxton, are called by Priam to
determine whether or not a truce is deemed advisable. To these
subsequent meetings, Shakespeare was obviously not indebted for
subject matter, nor to the first for the position he gave the episode
in the play, or for its subject matter. In the Iliades, however, the
second meeting of the Trojan council, in the time-sequence of
action, holds a place analogous to that in the play.[1] It is additional
evidence, not conclusive in itself, that Shakespeare was following
the Homeric pattern of events, and when we consider the similarity
in the subject matter of the council in the epic and in the drama,
the combined evidence is proof of Shakespeare's further debt to
the Iliades.

For in the epic, the subject of debate before the council is whether
or not to return Helen to Menelaus, and that is the argument in
Troilus and Cressida. In the other versions, the question is whether
or not to open hostilities against Greece, and once the decision for
war is passed, the best way to begin an aggressive policy is debated.

One is inclined to think that Shakespeare illustrated in the ideas
the Trojans express in this scene in the play Iris' description of
the kind of council that flourished in Ilium. "O Priam thou art al-
waies pleasde, with indiscrete aduice" [Iliades, p. 43]. Shakespeare

---

1. Shakespeare somewhat shifted the position of the council as it
occurs in the Iliades. In Troilus and Cressida, it takes place before
the Ajax-Hector combat; in the epic immediately after.

gives evidence of this indiscreet advice in the speeches Paris and
Troilus make. And Hector abandons his rational outlook and sides
with the younger men's proposals. The Trojan fall is entirely credible.
   In dramatizing the council scene, Shakespeare was unquestionably
indebted to Homer for subject matter, for the position or location
of the incident in the pattern of events, and for the kind of council
that was characteristic of the Trojans. The details that build up
the action, and the dialogue, are not exclusively Homeric, nor entirely "mediaeval," but are selections from accounts that Shakespeare combined with his characteristic felicity.
   In the Homeric account, Priam summons the council to pass on
a resolution proposed by Antenor that the Trojans return Helen
before it is too late. In the scenes described by Lydgate, Caxton,
and Heywood, Priam summons his council to determine whether
or not to re-open hostilities with Greece. In Troilus and Cressida,
Priam summons the council to answer Nestor's proposal. This
Greek negotiation is not Homeric. As it stands in the play, it has
no precedent anywhere. In the Lydgate-Caxton version of the siege,
however, Diomedes and Ulysses undertake an embassy to Troy,
before hostility begins, even before the main Greek force arrives
at Troy, to attempt by negotiation a peaceful settlement. Let Helen
be returned and the loot Paris stole from "Cythare" be restored,
and the Greeks will return to the homeland. The proposal is instantly
rejected by Priam, and the Greek ambassadors barely escape alive.
There is no debate, no weighing of consequences [Rec.II.558 ff.; AH,
481 ff.; Troy Book, II.6800 ff.]. This Greek proposal, made in person,
and at so early a date in the war, has been reduced in Troilus and
Cressida to a piece of correspondence, and shifted in time to accord
with the Homeric pattern of events.
   The characters who comprise the council in the Lydgate-Caxton
version, Shakespeare has taken over into the play, and to a degree
has retained in his characterization the points of view they hold
in a different situation. Hector, at first, and Helenus align themselves against Troilus and Paris in the play, as they do in the narrative. Shakespeare dropped Deiphobus from the scene (no doubt to
cut down the number of players), but it is permissible to think that
some of his philosophy has passed, in the play, into Troilus' re-
proach of Helenus. "Reason and respect," which "Make livers pale
and lustihood deject" is another way of saying "if in all the works
that men should beginne, they should be aduised euer in the particularities and singular things that might happen or fal, they should
neuer enterprise nor do valiant act by hardinesse" [Rec.II.522; AH, 450].
450].
   The close dependence that Shakespeare shows on the Caxton version is in his characterization of Hector in council. In the earlier
version, Hector first vigorously opposes an aggressive policy.
Hesione is not worth a war. The Greeks have too large an empire
and too many soldiers to seek entanglements with them. It is best
not to re-open hostility since the prospect of a Trojan victory is

uncertain. Hector abandons his stand, however, when he learns
that Hesione is held in subjection, and that Antenor's embassy
was not accorded due respect by the Greeks. In the play, Hector
is cautious. Helen, and not Hesione, is now not worth the cost
[II.ii.51 ff.]. One cannot be certain of victory. "Who knows what
follows?" [II.ii.13]. Nevertheless, Hector abandons his sane position for the honor and renown that championing Helen will bring
to his skill in arms.

Helenus, as he appears in the play, has undergone a change. In
the Caxton version, he is simply a prophet of doom. In the play
(his part is very small), he supports Hector's early view of the
situation, and stresses the necessity of a rational judgment in
decision. His philosophy provokes Troilus, who insults Helenus
and his profession which weakens hardihood. He is a seer and
prophet, or one "for dreams and slumbers." Reason, which Helenus
approves, is in reality only the shield to his cowardice. To talk
of reason is to evince "harehearts." Shakespeare retained the
spirit of Troilus' attack as it occurs in the Recuyell, but he also
made several changes. Helenus is labeled a coward in all versions
but, in the play, Shakespeare emphasizes reason as the excuse, or
cause of his timidity. Secondly, the priests' custom "to loue good
cheere and pleasures, & to fill their bellies with good wines and
with good meats" weakens in them desire for action. In Troilus
and Cressida, reason, according to Troilus, is the food that fattens
thought, and makes activity lean [II.ii.46 ff.].

Paris, at the time of the council in the early accounts, does not
possess Helen. She is still a dream. Shakespeare was not indebted
to Caxton for the part he has in the play. Paris, on the other hand,
is like his namesake in the Iliades, though Shakespeare developed,
apparently without others' suggestions, the reason why he should
keep Helen. Homer's Paris simply says he will.

Cassandra remains the same character in all accounts. In Shakespeare's play and in Heywood's, however, she interrupts the meeting,
and warns councillors against a foolish decision. In the other versions, her prophecy follows the decision.[2]

In the Iliades, Paris and Antenor are the only speakers in the
council. Shakespeare did not introduce Antenor into his play, but
his argument that to keep Helen is "to defend but broken faiths"
may be the suggestion for Hector's plea in the drama that "All
dues be render'd to their owners" [II.ii.46 ff.].

For the similar scene in the Iron Age, Heywood followed Lydgate
or Caxton, and his account is no improvement on the original. If
the Iron Age did precede Troilus and Cressida, Shakespeare found
nothing in it that led him to deviate from Caxton or Homer.

2. Also the prophecy is uttered in council in Peele's poem. Interestingly enough, Peele also turns the original council about revenging
Hesione to a council on the problem of returning Helen.

In the Trojan council scene in <u>Troilus and Cressida</u>, rational considerations are at war with desires for personal glory and honor. Characters that see the truth are Helenus and Hector: but finally Helenus is the sole opponent of the decision to keep Helen. Hector, stirred by Troilus above all, allows his better judgment to be darkened and his rational outlook overcome by expectation of fame. At the end of the scene, Hector, Paris, and Troilus stand out as "exempla" of great figures whose safer guides have been quite overmastered by their passions. In them, "the will dotes."

The humanistic theme that underlies the arguments is actually to be spotted in the similar scenes in all the sources. But Shakespeare has given it a real prominence in this scene, and has made Hector, the chief actor on the Trojan field, a counterpart of Achilles. As the judgment of Achilles is blinded by pride and self-esteem, and he declines into a confusion, a chaos, which threatens to destroy him and Greece, so Hector's judgment is blinded by a lust for personal fame that leads him and Troy to destruction. As Professor Campbell notes, Hector "yields his rational leadership to a democracy of conflicting wills and takes the fatal step which leads to the ruin of himself and his army."[3] Achilles and Hector, though of different race, are yet in one sense kith and kin.

3. O. J. Campbell, <u>Shakespeare's Satire</u>, p. 110.

THE LOVE STORY

15. *Troilus and Pandarus*

Shakespeare's version of the Troilus-Cressida plot is closer to Chaucer's than it is to any account of the story before 1602 which has survived.[1] It cannot, however, be stated without some reservation that Shakespeare had direct recourse to Chaucer's poem, and transferred the incidents which make up the plot from the poem to his play, since several dramas on Troilus and Cressida, now lost, existed, and were in all probability based on Chaucer's version. Shakespeare could have developed his plot from such an intermediate account.[2] Most writers in Elizabethan times were familiar with the general story of Troilus and Cressida [3] and, for so relatively simple a tale, could have worked up the material without having recourse to Chaucer's long poem. But the resemblances, both detailed and general, to Chaucer's poem that are evident in Troilus and Cressida incline one to think that Shakespeare was quite familiar with an edition of the poem. That is not to say that Shakespeare caught, or transmitted the spirit of the original, but in the main, he reproduced the form, or plot, faithfully. And frequently it is possible to locate the suggestion for his dialogue in the narrative. Certain deviations that Shakespeare

1. This entire section is, of course, indebted to R. S. Small's The Stage Quarrel (Boston, 1899).
2. See Tatlock for a discussion of this problem, PMLA, XXX (1915), 755 ff. His reconstruction of the "Admiral Fragment," from the surviving stage directions, is entirely reasonable, but, of course, enough of it does not exist to allow one to determine how faithfully the authors followed the Chaucer plot. For a translation of the Welsh play, and a discussion of it, see John S. P. Tatlock, "The Welsh Troilus and Cressida, and its relation to the Elizabethan Drama," MLR, X (1915), 265 ff. See also below, pp. 132–33.
3. Rollins has shown most completely how popular the story was in the sixteenth century, and why Shakespeare treated it as he did. Hyder E. Rollins, "The Troilus-Cressida Story, from Chaucer to Shakespeare," PMLA, XXXII (1917), 383 ff.

made from the original can be explained by the demands of the
dramatic medium, and by his over-all theme.

   When Shakespeare opens his play, Troilus is already suffering
from his love for Cressida. No reference is made in the opening
scene to the matter of the first book of Chaucer's poem, in which
is described the unsympathetic young man who only scoffs at others'
loves, nor to the fateful meeting of the lovers in the temple. When
the play opens, Troilus already has his passion, and his Pandarus.
He is a lover who has suffered much, and is impatient with Pandarus'
delay in procuring Cressida's love.

> Tro. Have I not tarried?
> Pan. Ay, the grinding; but you must tarry
> the bolting.
> Tro. Have I not tarried?
> Pan. Ay, the bolting; but you must tarry
> the leavening.
> Tro. Still have I tarried.
> Pan. Aye, to the leavening; but here's yet
> in the word "hereafter" . . . .
> Tro. Patience herself, what goddess e'er she be,
> Doth lesser blench at sufferance than I do. [I.i.17- 30]

   Chaucer's Troilus does not criticize Pandarus' devious policy
so openly. But Pandarus listens to several complaints.

> "But, Lord, how shall I doon? How shal I lyven?
> Whan shal I next my deere herte see?
> How shal this longe tyme awey be dryven,
> Til that thow be ayein at hire fro me?
> Thow maist answer, 'abid, abid,' but he
> That hangeth by the nekke, soth to seyne
> In gret disese abideth for the peyne." [4]   [II.981-87]

> But to Pandare alwey was his recours,
> And pitously gan ay to hym to pleyne,
> And hym bisoughte of reed and som socours:
> And Pandarus, that sey his woode peyne,
> Wex wel neigh ded for routhe, sooth to seyne,
> And bisily with al his herte caste
> Som of his wo to slen, and that as faste . . . .
>   [II.1352-58]

   Troilus' remarks to Pandarus in the play almost amount to a
comment on what his former self endured, "Have I not tarried?"
For though Chaucer's Troilus does not so openly tax Pandarus'
policy, nor reveal to him his impatience in so positive a way, his
impatience is certainly implied in his long and multiple wrestlings

---

   4. All quotations from the poem in the book are from The Complete Works of Geoffrey Chaucer, ed. F. N. Robinson (Boston
and New York, 1933).

with his passion. That was obvious enough to Shakespeare long
before he read of Troilus' first meeting with Criseyde.

For the play, Shakespeare chose to emphasize the impatient
strain in Troilus' nature, and he developed it, one might say, into
a ruling passion. His impulsiveness, his desire for immediate
fulfillment of what he desires, is manifest in several situations
in the play: in council, in the field, and in his love. And it is also
noteworthy that in each instance his impatience is increased by
the frequent baulking he receives, in council where his voice is
opposed by more seasoned thoughts, in the field where he is opposed
by more skillful fighters, and in his love for Cressida which can be
consummated only when Pandarus and she are ready.

Pandarus appears in the first scene of the play as a character
distinct from Chaucer's. In the poem, Shakespeare found no precedent for treating him as he did. In the poem, Pandarus never
attempts to increase Troilus' love for Criseyde by extolling her
virtues. He is bent on assuaging his passions. In the play, Pandarus
is a torment to Troilus. He incites the young man's passion, and
when ostensibly he tries to dispraise his niece, only praises her
the more.

> An her hair were not somewhat darker than Helen's,—
> well, go to,—there were no more comparison between the
> women: but for my part, she is my kinswoman; I would
> not, as they term it, praise her; but I would somebody
> had heard her talk yesterday, as I did: I will not dispraise
> your sister Cassandra's wit, but—   [I.i.43–49]

Such talk is no comfort to Troilus.

> O Pandarus! I tell thee, Pandarus,—
> When I do tell thee, there my hopes lie
>   drown'd,
> Reply not in how many fathoms deep
> They lie indrench'd. I tell thee I am mad
> In Cressid's love: thou answer'st, "she
>   is fair";
> Pour'st in the open ulcer of my heart
> Her eyes, her hair, her cheek, her gait,
>   her voice;
> But, saying thus, instead of oil and balm,
> Thou lay'st in every gash that love hath
>   given me
> The knife that made it.   [I.i.48–63]

Pandarus' reply to Troilus' criticism indicates that he feels his
efforts have merited nothing more than an affront. He is not totally
subservient to the wishes of Troilus, as is Chaucer's Pandarus.
He has a mind of his own, and threatens to meddle no further in
this business—an idea that never occurs to the early Pandarus, who
is as much a slave to Troilus' demand as Troilus is to Criseyde's
love.

Pan. . . . She's a fool to stay behind her father:
let her to the Greeks; and so I'll tell her the next
time I see her. For my part, I'll meddle nor make
nor more i' the matter.
Tro. Pandarus,—
Pan. Not I.
Tro. Sweet Pandarus,—
Pan. Pray you, speak no more to me! I will leave
all as I found it, and there's an end.
Tro. . . . .
But Pandarus—O Gods! how do you plague me.
I cannot come to Cressid but by Pandar;
And he's as tetchy to be woo'd to woo
As she is stubborn-chaste against all suit.   [I.i.87–104]

By accentuating Troilus' impatience, and by so altering Pandarus'
nature as to make him spar with, rather than simply to be the de-
voted aid to Troilus, Shakespeare created for his opening scene an
interplay of character, a conflict of temperaments—not an undesirable
situation for a first scene. The dramatist also added an unfamiliar
element to the well-known story when he made Pandarus declare
at the end of the scene that he will meddle no more in the business.
After his speech, in spite of Troilus' plea, he departs. It is very
likely that the dramatist was familiar with the dangers of an audience's reaction to "a twice told tale" and, to avoid their lethargy
or possibly something worse, took this liberty with his authority,
and concluded the scene with an unfamiliar ending, that would
certainly arouse speculation in the beholders.

Shakespeare's Troilus is anxious to keep from the court all
knowledge of his passion for Cressida, and the difficulty he has in
concealing his passion, he reveals to Pandarus.

At Priam's royal table do I sit;
And when fair Cressid comes into my thoughts,—
So traitor!—"When she comes!"—When is she thence?
. . . .
I was about to tell thee:—when my heart,
As wedged with a sigh, would rive in twain,
Lest Hector or my father should perceive me,
I have, as when the sun doth light a storm,
Buried this sigh in wrinkle of a smile . . . . [I.i.31–40]

Chaucer's Troilus is as scrupulous in keeping the secret. Many
times, the necessity for confining knowledge of the affair to the
actors is stressed, and in a sense, the need for secrecy causes
Troilus to remain inert when to act might prevent Criseyde's de-
parture to the Greeks [IV. 148 ff., 1569 ff.].

There is no situation comparable to Shakespeare's first scene
in the Recuyell, the Troy Book, or in the Iron Age. Pandarus plays
no active part in the Troilus-Cressida plots as narrated by Lydgate and Caxton, or as dramatized by Heywood. Lydgate discusses

the story in greater detail than do the other writers, but in his
account of Troilus' love for Cressida there is no reference to
Troilus' impatience and impetuousness.

> In a temple as he walked vp & doun,
> When he his ginnes and his hokis leide
> Amyd the eyen cerclid of Cryseyde,
> Whiche on that day he might[e] nat asterte:
> So thorugh his brest percrd & his herte,
> He went hym home, pale, sike, & wan.
> And in this wise Troylus first be-gan
> To be a seruaunt . . .
> Til he was holp aftir of Pandarus,
> Thorugh whose comforte & mediacioun,
> . . . .
> With gret labour first he cam to grace . . . .
>   [Troy Book, III.4208 ff.]

The trait in Chaucer's Troilus that Shakespeare chose to stress,
to point up in conversation in the first scene, indicates that he was
re-conceiving the same character as essentially passion ridden.
The complexity of Chaucer's Troilus has been reduced to a simplicity—desire impatient for gratification. What more love is to
the lover of the courtly romance, the seventeenth century Troilus
has no conception of. After the lapse of time, and through the
growth of new traditions, Chaucer's incomparable figure has become an exemplum of a devotee of the senses. What that leads to
his history in the play all too fully illustrates.

16. Pandarus and Cressida

Shakespeare's portrayal of Pandarus' attempts to arouse Cressida's affection for Troilus cannot be compared favorably with Chaucer's
several descriptions of the visits Pandarus pays his niece to prepare
her mind and emotions for the eventual acceptance of Troilus as
her lover. The relatively faster action that the play demands in the
development of an incident partly explains the differences in the
authors' treatment of substantially the same situation.[1] The rather
unusual conversation Pandarus and Cressida exchange, as they
stand in the street before Priam's palace (ostensibly to see the
return of the warriors from the plain below the city), in accent
and in the kind of humor, is in no direct descent from the conver-

1. R. A. Small, Stage Quarrel, p. 156, and Hamill Kenny, "Shakespeare's Cressida," Anglia, LXI (1937), 175, both note the harmful
effect the swift dramatic action has on the motivation and proper
development of character.

sation Chaucer's characters exchange under similar circumstances. But if not for the spirit, which primarily distinguishes it from Chaucer's, Shakespeare was indebted to the earlier author for the incidents that comprise the action of the scene.

Shakespeare has given Cressida a servant, Alexander, with whom she exchanges a few words and quips in the beginning of the scene, and for whom there is no precedent in extant accounts. Pandarus joins Cressida and "her man" while she is extolling Hector's prowess. Pandarus, who is much more inquisitive than his earlier namesake, wants to know what they were talking about before he arrived. As soon as he hears a brief report of the day's events, he puts Troilus into the conversation, with obvious intent on his part, even though conversation has not edged to his inclusion.

> . . . he'll [Hector will] lay about him to-day, I can tell
> them that: and there's Troilus will not come far behind;
> let them take heed of Troilus, I can tell them that too.
> [I.ii.57–61]

Pandarus attempts to worm a confession from Cressida that Troilus is superior to Hector. His extraordinary assertions do not win her agreement. All her replies are derisive when they are not evasive.

> Pan. . . . Troilus is the better man of the two.
> Cres. O Jupiter! there's no comparison.
> Pan. What! not between Troilus and Hector? Do
> you know a man if you see him?
> Cres. Ay, if I ever saw him before and knew him.
> Pan. Well, I say Troilus is Troilus.
> . . . .
> . . . No, Hector is not a better man than Troilus.
> Cres. Excuse me.
> . . . .
> Pan. Th' other's not come to't; you shall tell me
> another tale when th' other's come to't. Hector
> shall not have his wit this year.
> Cres. He shall not need it if he have his own.
> Pan. Nor his qualities.
> Cres. No matter.
> Pan. Nor his beauty.
> Cres. 'Twould not become him; his own's better.
> Pan. You have no judgment, niece . . . .   [I.ii.63–96]

It is entirely possible Shakespeare developed this dialogue from a passage that occurs in the second book of the poem. During his visit with his niece, Pandarus compares Hector and Troilus as knights without peer in the field and in fellowship. Though Pandarus does not attempt to dispraise Hector by praising Troilus, nor to discredit Hector by the comparison, yet by likening Troilus to Hector, and even by more fully detailing his merits than those of

his elder brother, Pandarus attempts to establish the idea of Troilus as a peerless lover, and one not to be refused. Only one man
in all Troy is his equal, and that is Hector.

> " But, by my trouthe, the kyng hath sones tweye,—
> That is to mene, Ector and Troilus,—
> That certeynly, though that I sholde deye,
> Thei ben as voide of vices, dar I seye,
> As any men that lyven under the sonne.
> Hire myght is wyde yknowe, and what they konne.

> " Of Ector nedeth it namore for to telle:
> In al this world ther nys a bettre knyght
> Than he, that is of worthynesse welle;
> And he wel moore vertu hath than myght.
> This knoweth many a wis and worthi wight.
> The same pris of Troilus I seye;
> God help me so, I knowe nat swiche tweye.

> . . . .

> " For yesterday, who so hadde with hym ben,
> He myghte han wondred upon Troilus;
> For nevere yet so thikke a swarm of been
> Ne fleigh, as Grekes fro hym gonne fleen,
> And thorugh the feld, in everi wightes eere,
> Ther nas no cry but 'Troilus is there!'

> " Now here, now ther, he hunted hem so faste,
> Ther nas but Grekes blood; and Troilus
> Now hym he hurte, and hym al down he caste;
> Ay where he wente, it was arayed thus:

> . . . .

> " Therto he is the frendlieste man
> Of grat estat, that evere I saugh my lyve,
> And wher hym lest, best felawshipe kan
> To swiche as hym thynketh able for to thryve."

[II.170–207]

Chaucer's Pandarus, one might say, raises up Troilus by likening
him to his matchless brother: Shakespeare's Pandarus builds up
Troilus by somewhat discrediting Hector's great repute. To associate Troilus with Hector is each Pandarus' method of impressing
Cressida with the true worth of Troilus. Shakespeare's Pandarus
becomes irked by Cressida's replies when they do not conform to
his own opinions. "You have no judgment, niece." Thereupon he
takes another tack, one that might be effective if Cressida were
a different kind of woman. He attempts to rouse her jealousy by
noting Helen's affection for Troilus. "She [Helen] prais'd his com-
plexion above Paris" [I.ii.103]. "I swear to you, I think Helen
loves him better than Paris . . . . Nay, I am sure she does. She
came to him th'other day in the compassed window . . ." [I.ii.113–16].
"But to prove to you that Helen loves him," [I.ii.126] Pandarus tells

a tale of this reputed love, which, for all its implications, would
arouse no one's jealousy, least of all Cressida's.

Chaucer has nothing of this in his story. Pandarus does not
attempt to hasten Criseyde's decision by rousing in her jealousy
of Helen's affection for Troilus. This appears to be Shakespeare's
addition to the story, as well as the sorry tale that Pandarus tells
as evidence.

So far Shakespeare's Pandarus has not been able to bring Cressida,
at least outwardly, to his way of thinking about Troilus. She fails
to note him worthier than Hector, or to show signs of resentment
of Helen's favor. When the troops return from the field, Pandarus
adopts more open tactics, and contrasts each of the warriors with
Troilus, not to the advantage, of course, of those he is contrasted
with.

> Pan. Here, here; here's an excellent place; here
> we may see most bravely. I'll tell you them all
> by their names as they pass by, but mark Troilus
> above the rest.
> . . . .
> That's Aeneas: is not that a brave man? he's one
> of the flowers of Troy, I can tell you: but mark
> Troilus; you shall see anon.
> . . . .
> That's Antenor: he has a shrewd wit, I can tell
> you: and he's a man good enough: he's one o' the
> soundest judgments in Troy, whosoever, and a
> proper man of person. When comes Troilus? I'll
> show you Troilus anon: if he see me, you shall
> see him nod at me.
> . . . .
> Yonder comes Paris, yonder comes Paris. Look
> ye yonder niece: is't not a gallant man too, is't
> not? . . . Would I could see Troilus now! you shall
> see Troilus anon.
> . . . .
> That's Helenus: I marvel where Troilus is. Hark
> do you not hear the people cry "Troilus"? . . .
> Cres. What sneaking fellow comes yonder?
> Pan. Where? yonder? that's Deiphobus. 'Tis
> Troilus! there's a man, niece! Hem! Brave Troi-
> lus! the prince of chivalry!
> . . . .
> Mark him; note him. O brave Troilus! Look well
> upon him, niece; look you how his sword is
> bloodied, and his helm more hacked than Hector's;
> and how he looks, and how he goes . . . . Had I a
> sister were a grace, or a daughter a goddess, he
> should take his choice . . . . Paris is dirt to him;

and, I warrant, Helen, to change, would give an
eye to boot.[2]   [I.ii.193-258]

As far as the evidence exists, Shakespeare constructed this
portion of the scene from Chaucer's less detailed description of
the Trojan fighters passing beneath Criseyde's window.

> But as she sat allone and thoughte thus,
> Ascry aros at scarmuch al withoute,
> And men cride in the strete, "Se, Troilus
> Hath right now put to flighte the Grekes route!"
> With that gan al hire meyne for to shoute,
> "A, go we se! cast up the yates wyde!
> For thorwgh this strete he moot to paleys ride;
> . . . ."
>
> This Troilus sat on his baye steede,
> Al armed, save his hed, ful richely;
> And wownded was his hors, and gan to blede,
> On which he rood a pas ful softely.
> But swich a knyghtly sighte, trewely,
> As was on hym, was nought, withouten faille,
> To loke on Mars, that god is of bataille.
> . . . .
>
> His helm tohewen was in twenty places,
> That by a tyssew heng his bak byhynde;
> His sheeld todasshed was with swerdes and maces,
> In which men myght many an arwe fynde
> That thirled hadde horn and nerf and rynde;
> And ay the peple cryde, "Here cometh oure joye,
> And, next his brother, holder up of Troye!" [II.610-44]

On a second occasion, Criseyde and Pandarus watch Troilus
go by, but Shakespeare's account is closer to Chaucer's first.
On which occasion, considerable mention is made of Troilus'
looks and manner, his hacked helmet, and the signs of battle
on the man, details Shakespeare transferred to the play, and
though significantly he placed Cressida in the street, and gave
her Pandarus' company (in the second window scene in the poem,
Pandarus is with his niece), the incidents of the scene are the
same in the play and poem. Chaucer's Pandarus, in the second
window scene, does not so obviously extol Troilus, but his praise
is implied. To present Troilus in a group that comprises the
best knights of the city, and to rob each of those knights of their
particular additions and give them to Troilus, is Shakespeare's
effective contribution to the scene.

2. In the Iliad, Book III, Helen identifies for Priam the Greek
warriors as they appear on the field. But Shakespeare's situation
is different, and the suggestion for it was doubtless prompted
by the incident Chaucer describes.

In the play, once the "eagles are gone," Cressida remarks that
"There is among the Greeks Achilles, a better man than Troilus."
This sally entirely misses the humorless Pandarus. He lectures
his niece on what a man should mean to her.

> "Well, well!" Why, have you any discretion? have you any
> eyes? Do you know what a man is? Is not birth, beauty,
> good shape, discourse, manhood, learning, gentleness,
> virtue, youth, liberality, and such like, the spice and salt
> that season a man?   [I.ii.271-76]

These are qualities that Chaucer's Troilus manifests in abundance.
   Throughout the second scene of the play, Pandarus has been
treated very badly by his niece, whose perception goes far beyond
his judgment. His painfully obvious attempts to win a word of favor
from her meet with no success. He finally believes she has no
discretion. But it is a mistake to think that Cressida believes
what she says about Troilus. She has been ridiculing Pandarus
and not Troilus throughout the conversation; ridiculing his painfully obvious attempts to build up Troilus in her regard. Her true
feelings about Troilus are clearly expressed in her soliloquy.

> Words, vows, gifts, tears, and love's full sacrifice,
> He [Pandarus] offers in another's enterprise;
> But more in Troilus thousand-fold I see
> Than in the glass of Pandar's praise may be.
> Yet hold I off. Women are angels, wooing:
> Things won are done; joy's soul lies in the doing:
> That she belov'd knows nought that knows not this:
> Men prize the thing ungain'd more than it is . . . .
>   [I.ii. 307-14]

   For her philosophy of love, Shakespeare may have found suggestion in an idea expressed by Chaucer's Criseyde, though the
dramatist has pointed it up. Criseyde prefers to satisfy Troilus'
love by sight alone, lest complete intimacy mark a finishing date
in their story.

> But theron was to heven and to doone.
> Considered al thing it may nat be;
> And whi, for shame; and it were ek to soone
> To graunten hym so gret a libertee.
> For pleynly hire entente, as seyde she,
> Was for to love hym unwist, if she myghte,
> And guerdon hym with nothing but with sighte.
>   [II.1289-95]

   For the ideas expressed in his scene, Shakespeare got no hint
from Lydgate, Caxton, or Heywood. Shakespeare, as a matter of
fact, need not have had recourse to any author other than Chaucer
for the details and incidents. Most of the material dramatized is

in the poem: what is not, except for the spirit of the piece,[3] appears
to be Shakespeare's addition, and that is little. The miscellaneous
references to events in the scene do not seem to derive from a
single composition but are scattered recollections from rather
wide reading.

17. Pandarus, Helen, Paris

The action of the Troilus-Cressida plot is not advanced by
the events that take place when Pandarus visits Paris, but the
character of Cressida is further revealed.

The purpose of Pandarus' visit to Paris is to solicit Paris
to be the one to offer an excuse to Priam that Troilus will not
be able to sup at the palace. "And, my lord, he desires you,
that if the king call for him at supper, you will make his excuse"
[III.i.79-81] Paris is suspicious. "What exploit's in hand? where
sups he to-night? . . . I'll lay my life, with my disposer Cressida"
[III.i.85-91]. Pandarus' reply, "No, no, no such matter; you are
wide" [III.i.92] does not convince anyone. Paris, however, promises
to shield his brother against inquiry.

Pandarus' reference tells of the progress of Troilus' love for
Cressida more by implication than by direct allusion. But aside
from this bit of information, the scene is primarily the occasion
of a display of wit, and, of course, no comparable situation can
be found in the poem. The necessity for an excuse, however, which
will account for Troilus' absences from festivities at court, is
mentioned by Chaucer. The need of keeping secret his love for
Criseyde, stressed throughout the poem by the actors concerned,
causes Troilus to seek an excuse in explanation of his expected
disappearances.

> And Troilus, that al this purveiaunce
> Knewe at the fulle, and waited on it ay,
> Hadde hereupon ek mad gret ordinaunce,
> And found his cause, and therto his aray,
> If that he were missed, nyght or day,
> Ther-while he was aboute this servyse,
> That he was gon to don his sacrifise,
>
> And moste at swich a temple allone wake,
> Answered of Apollo for to be . . . .   [III.533-41]

The need of an excuse to explain Troilus' absences from court,
is recognized by Chaucer and Shakespeare: the particular excuse
given is an elaborate construction in the poem, and not mentioned
in the play.

---

3. See Rollins for the best account of the historical tradition of
the poem which explains the "spirit" of the story, PMLA, (1917), 383 ff.

18. *Troilus, Pandarus, Cressida*

The many visits that Chaucer's Pandarus pays his niece, and
his many and long explanations why she should accept Troilus
as lover (all of which are masterly persuasions in the courtly
love tradition), are omitted from the play, as are Pandarus'
frequent reports to Troilus on the progress of his stratagem.
The fluctuations of the emotions Chaucer so skillfully handles
Shakespeare did not intend to reproduce on the stage. His hand
is heavier but of necessity so, since he was conceiving another
Troilus. To do it, he eliminated many psychological explorations
Chaucer made to round out his character, and concentrated rather
on the more obvious feelings of Troilus. For these reasons, when
Troilus gains Cressida's consent to be her lover in fact, and he
meets her in her own orchard, the incident comes as something
of a shock, but designedly so. Shakespeare's brief treatment of
the emotional states the characters pass through before Cressida's
surrender makes her appear as easy game, and Troilus as an
impatient sensualist. Shakespeare has, of course, developed their
affair so in order to underline its nature.

Shakespeare's Troilus is, as Professor Rollins pointed out,[1]
a sensualist—a suggestion that came, of course, from Chaucer's
delineation. Shakespeare has made the language much more expressive; the desire of Troilus more concentrated, intense. Impatient for Cressida's love, he complains to Pandarus:

> . . . I stalk about her door,
> Like a strange soul upon the Stygian bank
> Staying for waftage. O! be thou my Charon,
> And give me swift transportance to those
>   fields,
> Where I may wallow in the lily-beds
> Propos'd for the deserver.   [III.ii.8–13]

Chaucer's Troilus, after the night spent with Criseyde, exclaims
to Pandarus:

> . . . "O frend of frendes the alderbeste.
> That evere was, the sothe for to telle,
> Thow hast in hevene ybrought my soule at reste
> Fro Flegetoun, the fery flood of helle . . . ".
>   [III.1597–1600]

Troilus' speech in the play as he waits for Pandarus and
Cressida is properly cited as an example of his sensual nature.[2]

1. Rollins, PMLA, XXXII (1917), 383–84.
2. Ibid., p. 383.

> I am giddy, expectation whirls me round.
> The imaginary relish is so sweet
> That it enchants my sense. What will it be
> When that the watery palate tastes indeed
> Love's thrice repured nectar? death, I fear me,
> [Swounding] destruction, or some joy too fine,
> Too subtle-potent, tun'd too sharp in sweetness,
> For the capacity of my ruder powers . . . .
>   [III.ii.17-24]

Chaucer's Troilus experiences this "[swounding] destruction"
when he fears Criseyde will not satisfy his desires.

> The felyng of his sorwe, or of his fere,
> Or of aught elles, fled was out of towne;
> And down he fel al sodeynly a-swowne.   [III.1090-92]

Shakespeare's Pandarus works as arduously to bring Troilus
and Cressida together as does Chaucer's character, but the
dramatist has coarsened his speech and roughened his manners.

Cressida's confession of her love for Troilus is also found in
Chaucer's poem, in what is, making allowance for the demands
of stage decorum, the same situation.

> Boldness comes to me now, and brings me heart.
> Prince Troilus, I have loved you night and day
> For many weary months.   [III.ii.123-25]

> "Ne hadde I er now, my swete herte deere,
> Ben yolde, ywis, I were now nought heere!"
>   [III.1210-11]

Shakespeare concludes his scene with the lovers' formal
protestations of their faith one to another. The formal conclusion
is suggested by verses in the poem in which Troilus and Criseyde
protest unfailing love for each other.

> Tro. True swains in love shall in the world
>   to come
> Approve their truths by Troilus: when their
>   rimes,
> Full of protest, of oath, and big compare,
> Want similes, truth tir'd with iteration,
> As true as steel, as plantage to the moon,
> As sun to day, as turtle to her mate,
> As iron to adamant, as earth to the centre,
> Yet, after all comparisons of truth,
> As truth's authentic author to be cited,
> As true as Troilus shall crown up the verse
> And sanctify their numbers.
> . . . .
> Cres. . . . .
> If I be false, or swerve a hair from truth,
> When time is old and hath forgot itself,

When waterdrops hath worn the stones of Troy,
And blind oblivion swallow'd cities up,
And mighty states characterless are grated
To dusty nothing, yet let memory,
From false to false, among false maids in love,
Upraid my falsehood! when they've said "as
           false
As air, as water, wind, or sandy earth,
As fox to lamb, or wolf to heifer's calf,
Pard to the hind; or stepdame to her son,"
Yea, let them say, to stick the heart of
           falsehood,
"As false as Cressid."   [III.ii.185–208]

To this answerde Troilus and seyde,
"Now God, to whom ther nys no cause ywrye,
Me glade, as wys I nevere unto Criseyde,
Syn thilke day I saugh hire first with yĕ,
Was fals, ne nevere shal til that I dye.
At shorte wordes, wel ye may me leve:
I kan na more, it shal be founde at preve."
                                          [IV. 1653–59]

To that Criseyde answerde right anon,
And with a sik she seyde, "O herte deere,
The game, ywys, so ferforth now is gon,
That first shal Phebus fallen fro his spere,
And everich egle ben the dowves feere,
And everi roche out of his place sterte,
Er Troilus out of Criseydes hert."   [III.1492–98]

At a later date in the poem, in more extravagant terms, Criseyde
swears she will be true, and calls the gods to witness her oath
[IV. 1534 ff].

Shakespeare built up the suggestions for these speeches he
found in Chaucer into formal, balanced declarations of faith, and
added Pandarus as a witness to ratify and seal their oaths.

Heywood, in the Iron Age, devotes a few lines to Troilus and
Cressida, as lovers, in which scene they perform vows of love,
after a fashion.

Tro. Daughter to Calchus and the pride
            of Troy,
Plight me your hand and heart.
Cres. Faire Heauen I doe.
Will Troilus in exchange grant me his too?
Tro. Yes, and fast seal'd, you gods, your
            anger wreak
On him or her, that first this vnion breake.
Cres. So protests Cresida, wretched may
            they dye,
That 'twixt our soules these holy bands
            untye.   [Dr.Wks. III.288]

Very tenuous links exist in this instance between the <u>Iron Age</u> and <u>Troilus and Cressida</u>. Neither Lydgate nor Caxton, however, gives so much attention to this episode as Heywood. What Shakespeare wrote in dramatizing this scene can be found in Chaucer's poem: what cannot, for want of evidence, can be attributed to his conscious alteration, an alteration that makes Troilus as so infatuated with desire that his judgment has become blind. He cannot see Cressida as she is.

19. Calchas' Request

Shakespeare opens the third scene of the third act with Calchas' plea to the Greeks that they grant Cressida's exchange for Antenor.

> Now, princes, for the service I have done you,
> The advantage of the time prompts me aloud
> To call for recompense. Appear it to your mind
> That through the sight I bear in things of lore,
> I have abandon'd Troy, left my possession,
> Incurr'd a traitor's name; expos'd myself,
> From certain and possess'd conveniences,
> To doubtful fortunes; sequestering from me all
> That time, acquaintance, custom, and condition
> Made tame and most familiar to my nature . . . .
> [III.iii.1–10]

Chaucer's Calchas expresses the same ideas in different words, though he will forego the loss of treasure if he can have his daughter in recompense.

> Than seyde he thus, "Lo, lordes myn, ich was
> Troian, as it is knowen out of drede;
> And, if that yow remembre, I am Calkas,
> That alderfirst yaf comfort to youre nede,
> And tolde wel how that ye shulden spede.
> For dredeles, thorugh yow shal in a stownde
> Ben Troie ybrend, and beten down to grownde.
> . . . .
> And, for the Grekis weren me so leeve,
> I com myself, in my propre persone,
> To teche in this how yow was best to doone,
>
> Havyng unto my tresor ne my rente
> Right no resport, to respect of youre ese.
> Thus al my good I lefte and to yow wente,
> Wenyng in this yow, lordes, for to plese.
> But al that los ne doth me no disese.
> I vouchesauf, as wisly have I joie,
> For yow to lese al that I have in Troie,
>
> Save of a doughter that I lefte, allas!"   [IV. 71–92]

Caxton did not write of Calchas' request in any detail [Rec.II. 601-2; AH, 518 ff.]; Lydgate only states that Calchas wants his daughter. No reference is made to his sacrifices, or his valuables at Troy [Troy Book,III.3697 ff.].

In the Iron Age, Calchas persuades his daughter to depart with him to the Greek camp. He makes no formal request to Agamemnon that she be returned. Indeed, the exchange is not an episode in Heywood's play.

>   Cal.   In one word this Troy shall be sackt
>   and spoil'd
>   For so the gods haue told mee, Greece shall
>   conquer,
>   And they be ruin'd, leaue then iminent perill,
>   And flye to safety.
>   Cres. From Troilus?
>   Cal.   From destruction, take Diomed and liue,
>   Or Troilus and thy death.
>   Cres. Then Troilus and my ruine.
>   Cal.   Is Cresid mad?
>   Wilt thou forsake thy father, who for thee
>   And for thy safety hath forsooke his Countrey?
>   Cres. Must then this City perish?
>   Cal.   Troy must fall.
>   Cres. Alas for Troy and Troilus.
>   Cal.   Loue King Diomed.
>   . . . .
>   Be briefe, say quickly wilt thou? is it done?
>   Cres. Diomed and you i'le follow, Troilus shun.
>   [Dr.Wks. III.303-4]

20. The Exchange

Shakespeare opens the fourth act of his play with Diomedes' arrival in Troy. The enmity that flares up in the greetings exchanged by Diomedes and Aeneas, is not explained by any event that has taken place in the drama. The origins of the hostility between the two warriors is in an incident which occurred long before the action of Shakespeare's play begins. But he is referring to it in this scene. Caxton described the situation in the Recuyell.[1]

Before Agamemnon departed with his host from Tenedos, he sent Diomedes and Ulysses to Troy, as ambassadors, to try by peaceful means to persuade Priam to return Helen and make restitution for the damage Paris wrought during his stay in Greece. Priam, incensed by the many injuries the Greeks had inflicted

1. The embassy appears to have been a dramatic incident in the "Admiral Fragment." Diomedes, Menelaus, and Deiphobus were the ambassadors. See Tatlock, PMLA, XXX (1915), 698.

on his city and on his race in times past, received the ambassadors with scant civility. ". . . let Agamemnon knowe, that I desire
neuer to haue peace nor loue with the Greeks, that haue done to
me so many displeasures. And if it were not that ye be messengers,
I shoulde make you die an euill death. Therefore goe ye your way
anon . . ." [Rec.II.560; AH, 483 ff.; Troy Book, II.6751 ff.].

Diomedes shows his disdain of the Trojan king and insolently
laughs in his face:

> . . . Then beganne Diomedes to laugh for despight, and
> sayde thus: Ha king, if without displeasure thou mayest
> not see vs, that be but twaine, then wilt thou not be with-
> out displeasure all the dayes of thy life: for thou shalt
> see from hencefoorth before thine eyes great armies of
> Greekes, the which shall come before the citie, and shall
> not cease for to assaile it continually: against whom thou
> mayest not long defend thee, but that thou and thine
> finally shall receiue bitter death.[Rec.II.560-61; AH, 482-83]

This speech nearly costs the ambassadors their lives. "Then
were there many Troyans that would haue runne vppon the Greekes,
and drew their swordes for to haue slaine them. But the king
Priamus forbade them . ." [Rec.II.561; AH, 483]. Aeneas, before
all the councilors, takes it upon himself to answer Diomedes,
but his words only provoke further insolence from the haughty
Greek. Ulysses intercedes in good time.

> . . . Ha, ha, sir, sayd Eneas, what is that, that yee say?
> men must shewe to a foole his foolishnesse: and truely,
> if it were not in your presence, this fellow that hath
> spoken so foolishly before you, shoulde receiue his death
> by mine owne hande. It apperteineth not vnto him to say
> vnto you such vile and venemous wordes nor menaces:
> and therefore I aduise him, that he goe his way quickly,
> vnlesse he cease to speake foolishly. Diomedes, that of
> nothing was abashed, answered to Eneas and sayd: What-
> soeuer thou be, thou shewest well by thy words, that thou
> art right ill aduised, and hote in thy wordes: and I wish'
> and desire that I may once finde thee in aplace conuenient,
> that I may rewarde thee. for the wordes that thou hast
> spoken of me. I see well that the king is fortunate and
> happie to haue such a counsailer as thou art, and giueth
> him counsell to do villanie. Then Ulisses brake the words
> of Diomedes right wisely . . . .   [Rec.II.561-62; AH, 483-84]

The enmity Diomedes and Aeneas show to each other, and which
crops out when they exchange greetings in Troy in Shakespeare's
version, has its origins in this past event which Shakespeare was
remembering when he began his act—the altercation between
Aeneas and Diomedes.

> Aene.   Health to you, valiant sir,
> During all question of the gentle truce;

> But when I meet you arm'd, as black defiance
> As heart can think or courage execute.
> Dio.   The one and other Diomed embraces.
> Our bloods are now in calm, and, so long,
>   health!
> But when contention and occasion meet,
> By Jove, I'll play the hunter for thy life
> With all my force, pursuit, and policy.
> Aene. And thou shalt hunt a lion, that will
>   fly
> With his face backward. In humane gentleness,
> Welcome to Troy! now, by Anchises' life,
> Welcome, indeed! by Venus' hand I swear,
> No man alive can love in such a sort
> The thing he means to kill more excellently.
> Dio.   We sympathise. Jove, let Aeneas live,
> If to my sword his fate be not the glory,
> A thousand complete courses of the sun!
> But, in mine emulous honour, let him die,
> With every joint a wound, and that to-morrow!
> Aene. We know each other well.   [IV. i. 10–30]

As Paris, Aeneas, and Diomedes proceed on their way to ful-fill their mission, the scene shifts to the lovers. Troilus is lament-ing the arrival of day, and Cressida too has her objections to the morning.

> Tro. O Cressida! but that the busy day,
> Wak'd by the lark, hath rous'd the ribald crows,
> And dreaming night will hide our joys no longer,
> I would not from thee.
> Cres. Night hath been too brief.
> Tro.   Beshrew the witch! with venemous wights
>   she stays
> As tediously as hell, but flies the grasps of love
> With wings more momentary-swift than thought.
>   [IV. ii. 8–14]

A common refrain, the lovers' lament of the swiftness of night, and one that Chaucer's Troilus and Criseyde also voice on the same occasion, though in different accents, and without reference to the tediousness of night that "venemous wights endure." Criseyde is the first to speak against the day.

> "O nyght, allas! why nyltow over us hove,
> As longe as whan Almena lay by Jove." [III. 1427–28]

Troilus continues:

> "O cruel day, accusour of the joie
> That nyght and love has stole and faste
>   iwryen,
> Acorsed be thi comyng into Troye,
> For every bore hath oon of thi bryghte yĕn!
> Envyous day, what list the so to spien?

What hastow lost, why sekestow this place,
Ther God thi light so quenche, for his grace?

"Allas! what have thise loveris the agylt,
Dispitous day? Thyn be the peyne of helle!
For many a lovere hastow slayn, and wilt;
Thy pourynge in wol nowher lat hem dwelle.
[III. 1450-60]

Shakespeare's Troilus and Cressida have no more than a few
moments to themselves before Pandarus is stirring: "What! 's
all the doors open here?" [IV. ii. 19]. Not unnaturally Cressida
remarks, "A pestilence on him! now will he be mocking" [IV. ii.21].

Pan. How now, how now! how go maidenheads?
Here, you maid! where's my cousin Cressid?
Cres. Go hang yourself, you naughty mocking
                uncle!
You bring me to do—and then you flout me too.
Pan. To do what? to do what? let her say
                what:
What have I brought you to do?   [IV. ii.23-28]

Chaucer's Pandarus does not greet Criseyde the next morning
without alluding to the night before, though his reference is more
veiled.

Pandare, o-morwe which that comen was
Unto his nece, and gan hire faire grete,
Seyde, "Al this nyght so reyned it, allas,
That al my drede is that ye, nece swete,
Han litel laiser had to slepe and mete.
Al nyght," quod he, "hath reyn so do me wake,
That som of us, I trowe, hire hedes ake."

An ner he com, and seyde, "How stant it now
This mury morwe? Nece, how kan ye fare?"
Criseyde answerde, "Nevere the bet for yow,
Fox that ye ben! God yeve youre herte kare!
God help me so, ye caused al this fare,
Trowe I," quod she, "for al youre wordes white.
O, whoso seeth yow, knoweth yow ful lite." [III. 1555-68]

In the play, Pandarus' jesting is stopped by a knocking at the
courtyard gate. Aeneas enters and when he encounters Troilus,
breaks the heavy news to him.

Aene. My lord, I scarce have leisure to salute
                you,
My matter is so rash: there is at hand
Paris your brother, and Deiphobus,
The Grecian Diomed, and our Antenor
Deliver'd to us; and for him forthwith,
Ere the first sacrifice, within this hour,
We must give up to Diomedes' hand
The Lady Cressida.

Tro. Is it concluded so?
Aene. By Priam and the general state of Troy:
They are at hand and ready to effect it.   [IV. ii.62 – 71]

In Chaucer's version, Troilus is not suddenly confronted with
the decision taken by Priam and the state of Troy. He is present
when the council meets and knows beforehand the issue of debate.
His fear is primarily that Antenor will be deemed of more worth
to the city than Criseyde. As her secret lover, however, he dare
not raise his voice for or against her stay.

This Troilus was present in the place,
When axed was for Antenor Criseyde;
For which ful soone chaungen gan his face,
As he that with tho wordes wel neigh deyde.
But natheles he no word to it seyde,
Lest men sholde his affeccioun espye . . .
. . . .
Love hym made al prest to don hire byde,
And rather dyen than she sholde go;
But resoun seyde hym, on that other syde,
"Withouten assent of hire ne do nat so,
Lest for thi werk she wolde be thy fo,
And seyn that thorugh thy medlynge is iblowe
Youre bother love, ther it was erst unknowe."
[IV. 148 – 68]

The decision of the council does not occur the morning after
the first night Troilus and Criseyde spend together. Troilus'
passion has more than the one night's satisfaction [III. 1716 ff.],
and he is able "in blisse" "al his life to lede."

Shakespeare, in adapting the same situation to the play, has
not dramatized the action of the council. It is described as having
met and passed its decision which Aeneas, the official informer
of plans in Troy, reports to Troilus. Troilus himself knows
nothing about the action until Aeneas suddenly confronts him with
the news.

For reasons of economy, Shakespeare may have decided against
dramatizing the council. Or, more likely, he may have foreseen
a chance to heighten the drama by keeping Troilus in ignorance
until Aeneas suddenly appears with the decision reached by the
council. The joy Troilus and Cressida express in the opening of
the scene is stopped by the sudden knocking at the gate, and
Aeneas' revelation turns all joy to sorrow. Shakespeare, it seems
more than likely, purposely altered the original story in such a
fashion in order to gain strong emotional contrasts.

In the play, Pandarus breaks the news to Cressida that she must
leave Troy and join her father. She refuses to go.

I will not, uncle: I have forgot my father;
I know no touch of consanguinity;
No kin, no love, no blood, no soul so near me

As the sweet Troilus. O you gods divine!
Make Cressid's name the very crown of
          falsehood
If ever she leave Troilus!   [IV. ii. 102–7]

Chaucer's Criseyde first hears a rumor that she is to be exchanged, which is later confirmed by the women of Troy [IV. 680 ff.].
In her grief, she also swears to the gods to be true, and regards
no one in like esteem with Troilus.

" For thilke day that I for cherisynge
   Or drede of fader, or of other wight,
   Or for estat, delit, or for weddynge,
   Be fals to yow, my Troilus, my knyght,
   Saturnes doughter, Juno, thorugh hire
               myght,
   As wood as Athamante do me dwelle
   Eternalich in Stix, the put of helle!

" And this on every god celestial
   I swere it yow, and ek on ech goddesse,
   On every nymphe and deite infernal,
   On satiry and fawny more and lesse,
   That halve goddes ben of wildernesse;
   An Attropos my thred of life tobreste,
   If I be fals! now trowe me if you leste!" [IV. 1534–47]

In the play, when Troilus returns for Cressida, he holds the
gods responsible for this separation. They are envious of their
love.
          Tro. Cressid, I love thee in so strain'd a
                    purity,
          That the bless'd gods, as angry with my fancy,
          More bright in zeal than the devotion which
          Cold lips blow to their deities, take thee
                    from me.
          Cres. Have the gods envy?
          Pan. Ay, ay, ay, ay; 'tis too plain a case. [IV. iv. 24–29]

Chaucer's Troilus sees Fortune's envious eye turned on their
happiness.
          " Allas, Fortune! if that my lif in joie
             Displesed hadde unto thi.foule envye,
             Why ne haddestow my fader, kyng of Troye,
             Byraft the lif . . . ?"   [IV. 274–77]

In the play, Troilus utters his fears that Cressida, subject to
the wiles of the Greeks, will weaken and forget him. He hasn't
the grace they possess.
          The Grecian youths are full of quality;
          They're loving, well compos'd with gifts
                    of nature,
          And flowing o'er with arts and exercise:
          How novelties may move, and parts with
                    person,

Alas! a kind of godly jealousy,
Which, I beseech you, call a virtuous sin,
Makes me afeard.
. . . .
In this I do not call your faith in question
So mainly as my merit: I cannot sing,
Nor heel the high lavolt, nor sweeten talk,
Nor play at subtle games; fair virtues all,
To which the Grecians are most prompt
          and pregnant:
But I can tell that in each grace of these
There lurks a still and dumb-discoursive
          devil
That tempts most cunningly! But be not
          tempted.
. . . .
Whiles others fish with craft for great
          opinion,
I with great truth catch mere simplicity;
Whilst some with cunning gild their copper
          crowns,
With truth and plainess I do wear mine bare.
Fear not my truth; the moral of my wit
Is "plain and true"; there's all the reach of it.
                                        [IV. iv. 76 - 108]

In similar words, Chaucer's Troilus warns Criseyde against the
Greeks, and contrasts Trojan rudeness with their grace.

" Ye shal ek seen so many lusty knyght
Among the Grekis, ful of worthynesse,
And ech of hem with herte, wit, and myght
To plesen yow don al his bisynesse,
That ye shul dullen of the rudenesse
Of us sely Troians, but if routhe
Remorde yow, or vertu of youre trouthe." [IV. 1485-91]

Shakespeare concludes his scene with the entrance of Diomedes,
who is ready to return Cressida to her father. He ignores Troilus'
initial greeting, and promptly calls on Cressida for her friendship.

                    Fair Lady Cressid
So please you, save the thanks this prince
          expects:
The lustre in your eye, heaven in your cheek,
Pleads your fair usage; and to Diomed
You shall be mistress, and command him
          wholly.   [IV. iv. 116 -20]

Troilus, if he discovers she has not this "fair usage," promises
to slay Diomedes "Though the great bulk Achilles be thy guard"
[IV. iv. 128]. Chaucer's Troilus, though he accompanies Criseyde
to the spot where the prisoners are to be exchanged, speaks no

word to Diomedes [IV.85 ff.]. Diomedes, however, offers his friendship to Criseyde, and swears to be her knight.

> " And by the cause I swor yow right, lo, now,
> To ben youre frend, and helply, to my myght,
> And for that more aquayntaunce ek of yow
> Have ich had than another straunger wight,
> So fro this forth, I pray yow, day and nyght,
> Comaundeth me, how soore that me smerte,
> To don al that may like unto youre herte . . . ."
>
> [V. 127–33]

Caxton devotes little space to the events leading to the separation of Troilus and Cressida. From his account, Shakespeare
would not have been able to get enough information to construct
his scenes as they now stand. Caxton notes, however, that Diomedes
exchanged words with Cressida when he returned with her to her
father's tent.

> . . . when he sawe her so faire and in riding by her side
> hee shewed to her all his minde, and made to her many
> promises, and especially desired her loue: and then
> when she knew the minde of Diomedes, she excused her,
> saying, that she would not agree to him, nor refuse
> him at that time, for her heart was not disposed at that
> time to answere otherwise. Of this answere Diomedes
> had great ioy. . . .   [Rec.II.604; AH, 521]

Lydgate is no more expressive: only more verbose [Troy Book,
III.4418 ff.]. Heywood has no comparable situation in the Iron Age.

21. Diomedes, Cressida, Troilus

In the poem, Chaucer does not introduce Criseyde to the Greek
leaders when she arrives in their camp. The scene as it stands
in the play appears to be Shakespeare's addition to the story,
though if he read Caxton closely he would have noted how pleased
the Greek leaders were to have her among them, how they feasted
her and gave her presents, for the purpose, however, of gaining
information on the state of things in Troy.

> The comming of Briseyda pleased much to all the
> Greekes, and they came thither and feasted her, and
> demaunded of her tidinges of Troy, and of the king
> Priamus, and of them that were within, and shee said
> vnto them as much as she knewe, courteously . . . .
> and there was none of them, but gaue to her a iewell
> at the departing . . . .   [Rec.II.605–6; AH, 522]

At the end of the scene in the play in which Cressida is introduced
to the Greeks, Ulysses is able to state that Diomedes is suffering

from Cressida's love.[1] Troilus has asked where Cressida is staying:

> At Menelaus' tent, most princely Troilus:
> There Diomed doth feast with him to-night;
> Who neither looks upon the heaven nor earth,
> But gives all gaze and bent of amorous view
> On the fair Cressid.
>
> . . . .
>
>   . . . of what honour was
> This Cressida in Troy? Had she no lover there
> That wails her absence?   [IV. v. 279–89]

In the poem, Diomedes wonders if Criseyde has a Trojan lover.
Considering the possibility, he is cautious in his first approaches
[V. 778 ff.].

The last major scene in the Troilus and Cressida story which
Shakespeare dramatized, Cressida's acceptance of Diomedes
while her disillusioned Trojan lover looks on helpless, shows
dependence on, and at the same time independence of, Chaucer's
version. In the poem, Troilus gets no closer to the Greek camp
than the wall of Troy where, watching the road below, he expects
Criseyde to appear [V. 1191 ff.]. His doubts and uncertainties as
to her fate are prolonged over a considerable period of time, and
not until he discovers the brooch Deiphobus struck from Diomedes'
clothing, is he convinced of her apostasy.

Shakespeare of necessity reduces Troilus' period of waiting
and uncertainty. Also, he makes him an eyewitness of Cressida's
unfaith. By introducing Troilus into the Greek camp, Shakespeare
joined his two plots on a common ground. Also, he gained an extraordinary dramatic situation which would have been wanting
had Troilus lamented his loss in single scenes, and Diomedes
and Cressida declared their love apart. Very likely Shakespeare
rearranged the events he found in his source because he saw an
opportunity of building up an effective and rather striking situation
which would end the love story on a dramatic level.[2] Though the

---

1. By reckoning, Cressida yields to Diomedes the first night
she spends in the Grecian camp. Rapid dramatic action, and
its consequences, help convince one that Cressida's love is
more mercurial than even Lydgate, quoting Guido, deemed.—
Troy Book, III. 4336 ff.

2. Fleay's explanation does not take into account the dramatic
advantages Shakespeare gained by so altering the original story.
"I believe that Shakespeare followed Chaucer, as his only authority, in his first sketch, and so did not take Troylus to the
Greek tents at all: this scene being given between Diomed and
Cressida only to show that Troylus' suspicion from the brooch
was a true one. But finding afterwards how easily he could make
him see instead of suspect by sending him with Hector to the
Greek tents, he cut out the fighting scene and the brooch, and

performance Cressida and Diomedes put on is more like a dumb
show for Troilus to descant upon than a well-developed situation,
it makes its point.

Cressida gives her sleeve to Diomedes as does her namesake
in the poem [V. 1042–43],[3] and the conclusion of the story is the
same in both accounts. Troilus laments that so fine a love can
wear so different an aspect in so short a time [V. ii. 133 ff.]. His
desire becomes a lust for revenge on Diomedes.

> Ay, Greek; and that shall be divulged well
> In characters as red as Mars his heart
> Inflam'd with Venus: never did young man
>   fancy
> With so eternal and so fix'd a soul.
> Hark, Greek: as much as I do Cressid love,
> So much by weight hate I her Diomed;
> That sleeve is mine that he'll bear in his
>   helm;
> Were it a casque compos'd by Vulcan's
>   skill,
> My sword should bite it.   [V. ii. 159–67]

>   You vile abominable tents,
> Thus proudly pight upon our Phrygian plains,
> Let Titan rise as early as he dare,
> I'll through and through you! And, thou great-
>   siz'd coward,
> No space of earth shall sunder our two hates . . . .[4]
>   [V. x. 23–27]

That too, aside from death is all Chaucer's Troilus desires: the
opportunity to take revenge on Diomedes.

> "Now God," quod he, "me sende yet the grace
> That I may meten with this Diomede!
> And trewely, if I have myght and space,
> Yet shal I make, I hope, his sydes blede . . . ."
>   [V. 1702–5]

The letter that Shakespeare's Cressida sends to Troilus [V. iii.
109 ff.]—though the contents are not divulged—is presumably not
unlike that Chaucer's Criseyde sends to Troilus [V. 1590 ff.]. In
the play, Troilus has seen enough of Cressida's actions to know

---

put in the additions to this scene." —F. G. Fleay, "On Certain
Plays of Shakespeare," Transactions of the New Shakespeare
Society, II (1874), 311.

3. The sleeve figures in Peele's Tale of Troy in The Dramatic
and Poetical Works of Robert Greene and George Peele, ed.
Alexander Dyce (London, 1861), p. 555.

4. Cf. Recuyell, II.644; AH, 556: ". . . Agamemnon made the
hoste approche neere to the Citie. and there pight their Tentes."
Cf. Quarto "pitcht"; Folio "pight."

what her words mean: in the poem he still has hope that some truth is expressed in the vague words.

Heywood treated the Troilus-Cressida story with such dispatch that Shakespeare could not possibly have found his treatment useful to his own.[5] Lydgate and Caxton devote more space to the Cressida-Diomedes aspect of the plot than to the Troilus-Cressida phase, but neither Lydgate nor Caxton[6] has anything to suggest to the dramatist that Chaucer had not revealed in greater detail.

It is not necessary to assume the existence of a lost play to account for the Troilus-Cressida plot in Shakespeare's play. The dramatist followed the outline of Chaucer's story, and the incidents that make up the story, with a fidelity that would appear slavish if the manner of interpreting the situations were not so different. To construct his plot, Shakespeare need not have turned to an author other than Chaucer.[7]

The very great similarities that exist between incidents in the poem and play do not, however, allow us to forget the equally great differences in characterization. Shakespeare has portrayed Cressida from the start as a prostitute. By her words, and the words of others—their like is not to be met with in the poem—her nature is clearly revealed. Her conversation with her uncle while the pair wait for Troilus to return from the battle, suggests her type; Paris does not deny the impression she first makes on us; Ulysses is outspoken. But Troilus is blind to what she is. He alone fails to spot her as a daughter of the game. Ulysses characterizes her the first time he sees her.[8]

5. Diomedes and Troilus quarrel about the "fair" seizure of Troilus' horse (Dr.Wks. III.305–6). Diomedes' seizure of Troilus' horse is an episode in Shakespeare's play (V.v. 1 ff.). Chaucer alludes to the incident (V. 1036), also Lydgate (III.4624 ff.) and Caxton (II.608; AH.524). Professor G. Blakemore Evans calls the writer's attention to the scene in the Iron Age (Dr.Wks. III.363–66) where Diomedes overhears Sinon's seduction of Cressida—a suggestion Heywood possibly got from Shakespeare's scene.

6. Troy Book, III.4850 ff., IV. 2132 ff.; Recuyell, II.608 ff., 610; AH, 520 ff., 524 ff.

7. Dramatists might produce several plays on one subject, but examples of an Elizabethan dramatist's following an earlier drama in detail and general outline are understandably wanting. In spite of their titles, the earlier Troilus-Cressida plays may have been no closer to Shakespeare's than is Heywood's episode.

8. Hamil Kenny thinks Ulysses' speech (IV.v. 55 ff.) is inserted to prepare the way for Cressida's suddenly changed character, which she reveals in the first scene in which she is alone with Diomedes.—Anglia, LXI (1937), 167. But Cressida is the same in Troy as in the Greek camp.

Shakespeare so portrayed Cressida, and allowed others to see her as a wanton, and not Troilus, in order to emphasize in Troilus how ardor can blind the judgment. In his passion, he mistakes assumed virtue for the real. A terrible disillusionment, of course, is the only conclusion to his story. Note too that the Troilus of the love affair is very much the Troilus of the Council Scene. His advice to the Trojans is distinguished for its eloquence and its folly. In his ardor he urges a course of action that marks a darkened judgment. Destruction is an inevitable conclusion.

Shakespeare kept the spirit of the post-Chaucerian conception of Cressida, and heightened the picture of Troilus as a youth, in love and war, characterized more by passion than discretion and perception, in order to intensify the idea that pervades every part of the drama that the judgments of major figures are corrupted by passions of one kind or another. Either death or dissolution results. Troilus becomes bitter after the truth dawns on him— revengeful as a result of his experience. There must be no pity, he tells Hector; he himself lives only for revenge [V. iii. 37 ff.].

CHAPTER IV:
SUMMARY AND CONCLUSIONS

22. *Shakespeare's Debt to His Authors*

23. *Relationship of Troilus & Cressida*

   to the Tragedies

SUMMARY AND CONCLUSIONS

22. Shakespeare's Debt to His Authors

"The important point to emphasize, once more, is that in the plotting . . . in the camp-scenes . . . Shakespeare was fully under the influence of mediaeval rather than classical conceptions of the tale of Troy."[1] Such is W. W. Lawrence's partial summary of Shakespeare's debt to his authors. But the statement needs revision. For there is good reason to believe that the eight books of the Iliades that Chapman published in 1598 were the basis of Shakespeare's siege plot, and that the dramatist, in constructing his play, built the action on the major events of the epic. He extends the action over precisely that period and crisis of the war contained in that part of the Iliades that was available to him, beginning from the withdrawal of Achilles and ending with his return to slay Hector. Shakespeare drew on the material of Books I and II of the Iliades, then skipped to the incidents of Book VII for the challenge and combat (passing over the matters of the untranslated third, fourth, fifth, and sixth books), and thence to the ninth and eleventh books.[2] The incidents as they appear in these few books became the substance of the siege plot of Troilus and Cressida. It appears that Shakespeare dramatized as much of the Iliades as he knew, omitting those incidents that could not be worked into the action.

But the mediaevalists were by no means overlooked. Caxton, more probably than Lydgate,[3] supplemented certain scenes Shakes-

---

1. William W. Lawrence, Shakespeare's Problem Comedies, p. 157.
2. Though Books VIII, X, and XVIII were translated by Chapman, Shakespeare could not make use of the incidents in them.
3. Elizabeth Stein, "Caxton's Recuyell and Shakespeare's Troilus," MLN, XLV (1930), 144-46, indicates in her research that had Shakespeare followed Lydgate rather than Caxton, at least one episode and several phraseological similarities would be missing from the play.
      In 1555, Thomas Marshe published the last edition of Troy Book before the turn of the century. Caxton's prose version ran through five printed editions from 1475 until 1607. About five years before Shakespeare wrote his play, Fiston, in 1596, it will be recalled, revised the Recuyell.

137

peare took from Homer, and suggested details that the dramatist used with varying success.[4] Achilles' love for Polyxena as an additional motive for his secession Shakespeare introduced from the Recuyell. The reason Hector breaks off combat with Ajax is Caxton's [see above, Section 6]. Hector's visit to the Greek camp is also derived from Caxton [see above, Section 7]. The dramatist's treatment of Hector's farewell, though it is no reproduction of Lydgate's or Caxton's scene, bears no resemblance to Homer's account, which Shakespeare was not familiar with [see above, Section 8]. The circumstances surrounding Hector's death are derived from the Recuyell [see above, Section 9], as are certain features in Shakespeare's presentation of the Trojan council scene [see above, Section 14].

The multifarious material in Troilus and Cressida does not appear to me to be the "jumble" that it is to Brander Mathews who thinks little is to be said for the form or structure of the play.[5] Nor is there, I think, a lack of a theme or "principle unifying" the incidents.[6] It seems to me that the theme is very evident, as it is exemplified in the natures and actions of the characters, and that all parts of the drama are held together by it. Each warrior—Achilles, Hector, Troilus—is clearly conceived as a man whose judgment in certain situations is overcome by passion. The judgment of Achilles is blinded by pride; Hector's by love of personal fame and glory; Troilus' judgment is so overcome by infatuation that he mistakes Cressida for a paragon. In council too, he is as blind as in love. He ignores and urges others to ignore what reason demands—that the laws of nature and of nations be preserved. Since, however, Achilles, Hector, and Troilus are different in temperament, there is no sameness in the characterization; and since their stories are unlike, the play has variety of action, but the drama leaves a unified impression because of a common failing in each of the principal actors.[7]

Traditional though the unifying theme is—the Passion-Judgment theme, and common in the works of Shakespeare's contemporaries—it probably came into Troilus and Cressida—and embraced material not in any source connected with it, that is, the love story—from Chapman's translation, since in that work the Passion-Judgment struggle is played up. It is not a gross exaggeration to say that

4. His introduction of Polyxena is not successful, nor is the deus ex machina in the form of Hecuba's letter, even though the actions connected with them depict the decline of Achilles.
5. Brander Matthews, Shakespeare as a Playwright (New York, 1913), p. 230.
6. O. J. Campbell, Comicall Satyre and Shakespeare's Troilus and Cressida (San Marino, 1938), pp. 189–90.
7. See Robert K. Presson's "The Structural Use of a Traditional Theme in Troilus and Cressida," PQ, XXXI (1952), 180–88.

Homer, through Chapman, became a sixteenth century humanist tract.

But Shakespeare's dependence on the Iliades was not solely confined to the plotting, and to the theme. He followed Homer's lead in characterization, and for the most part with success. The characters in the Recuyell have little vitality or individuality, and though to Shakespeare they may have had more reality than they appear to have for modern readers, it is not likely they would have made so strong an impression on his mind as the Homeric figures Chapman described.

Shakespeare's knowledge of Homer's Greeks was confined to the characteristics they reveal in the eight books Chapman translated. Since characters such as Menelaus, Patroclus, and Ajax are so briefly treated in those books, it is not surprising that Shakespeare delineated them more sketchily and with less vigor than Homer had. The dramatist's portraiture does not go far beyond the most obvious traits of character presented by their brief appearances in the epic. Menelaus is no other than the deserted husband. His part in the action and his voice in council do not measure up to the magnitude of his loss. Patroclus' passion for Achilles is about all Shakespeare could gather from his depiction in Chapman's version. Though the character of Ajax is derived from no known source, Alexander's description of the warrior [I.ii.19 ff.] is most likely derived from the pompous figure that appears in Book VII of the epic.[8] In the play he is amusingly described by Thersites who notes that he imitates Achilles in his pride, and is so blinded by it that he does not see reality. In such a frame of mind he mistakes Thersites for Agamemnon.

> The man's undone for ever; for if Hector break not
> his neck i' the combat, he'll break't himself in vain-
> glory. He knows not me: I said "Good morrow, Ajax";
> and he replies "Thanks, Agamemnon". What think you
> of this man that takes me for the general? He's grown
> a very land-fish, languageless, a monster. A plague
> of opinion!   [III.iii.259–67]

Here Achilles' problem is reflected in another, and how clearly Achilles is revealed in Ajax!

Paris is a minor figure in the play, and Helen does not appear at all in the translation— so no resemblance to the Homeric character would be expected. Her brief appearance in the play is "consistent with, if it is not explained by, the absence in these seven

---

8. R. A. Small, Stage Quarrel, p. 167. Shakespeare's Ajax is no closer to Ovid's (Metamorphoses, xiii) than he is to Sir John Harrington's The Metamorphosis of Ajax (London, 1595). Tatlock discusses the character at some length, PMLA, XXX (1915), 727 ff. Cp. Shakespeare's and Homer's description of Briareus (Iliades, pp. 13–14; Troilus and Cressida, I.ii.30–31).

books of even the outline of her character as given by Homer." [9]
Doubtless it is not without reason nor without significance that
these characters are the least Homeric in the play. [10]

In the poem and drama, Agamemnon is not a too successful
leader of men. Ever conscious of dissatisfaction in his command,
he does not have the power to amend it. Shakespeare has not degraded Agamemnon nor diminished his stature. In a sense he has
suppressed the sensual and covetous nature of the Homeric leader
by not showing these traits through action, but only by report,
and mostly by Thersites'. Ulysses in both is the power behind the
scenes and the true ruler of the army: ". . . in counsaile doth,
for chiefe director serue" [Iliades, p. 28]. In the play he is the
councilor who not only perceives the cause of weakness in Agamemnon's policy but takes steps to correct it—in the best tradition of Homer's Greek. Shakespeare simply expanded the nature
of the epic hero.

Though Nestor is a faithful dramatization of Homer's old
warrior, Shakespeare transferred to Ulysses much of the governing power he has in the epic. But in his habit of reminiscence he
is surely Homeric [Iliades, pp. 10, 50; Troilus and Cressida, IV.
v. 196-210]. Even the picture of Nestor arming for a night alarm
is suggested by Homer. Shakespeare's Achilles urges Patroclus
to mimic him:

> And then, forsooth, the faint defects of age
> Must be the scene of mirth; to cough and spit,
> And with a palsy-fumbling on his gorget,
> Shake in and out the rivet . . . .   [I.iii.172-75]

lines doubtless suggested by those Diomedes addresses to Nestor
in the epic:

> If my Lance dote with the defects, that fayle best
>   minds in age,
> Or find the Palsey in my hands, that doth thy life
>   engage . . . .   [p. 62]

Achilles' pride is Homeric, as is his love for Patroclus. As
the most insubordinate of the host, he is Homeric. "Thou still
art bittrest to my rule, contention and sterne flight To thee, are
vnitie and peace" [p. 7]. Thersites is Homer's character "copi-
ously dramatized." [11]

These characters, most completely developed in Chapman's

9. J. Foster Palmer, "Ethics from Homer to Christ," Transactions of the Royal Society of Literature, 2nd Series, XV
(1893), 80. A much neglected essay.

10. Shakespeare did not do much with Diomedes' character before
he appears in Troy to take Cressida to her father. He transferred
his activities, for the most part following Chaucer, to the Troilus-
Cressida plot.

incomplete translation—they are shades when they do appear in
the mediaeval histories—are also the most completely and faithfully presented by Shakespeare.

The action of the Troilus-Cressida love story duplicates that
of Chaucer's poem. In each, the plot begins with Troilus' love
for Cressida and ends with her submission to Diomedes. The episodes in the play that describe the progress and degeneration of
their passion can be paralleled in most instances with those in
the poem.

The depth Cressida had fallen to in his time Shakespeare ac-
cepted, but subtly he changed Troilus' character so that the four-
teenth century courtly lover emerges in the seventeenth century
as a youth so headstrong in his passion, and so blinded by it, that
he cannot see what Cressida is. Disillusionment is inevitable.

The suggestion to combine the love story and the siege plot
may have come from plays or from the chronicles, but in any
case Shakespeare has united the two plots by a common theme
—and one that has a strong humanistic bent. While the different
stories and situations and the many characters add diversity to
the play, the theme, revealed in the actions of each of the princi-
pals—Hector, Achilles, Troilus—perfectly unites all parts. In each
character, "the will dotes."

It seems to me, then, that Shakespeare knew Chapman's ren-
dition of Homer better than has usually been indicated. The dramatist's debt to the incomplete 1598 edition of Homer is manifest,
I think, in the central situation, in the episodes, in narrative flavor,
theme or conception, and in characterization.

23. Relationship of Troilus & Cressida to the Tragedies

Except in some recent studies,[1] what distinguishes comments
on Troilus and Cressida is the tendency of scholars to see the
play as a peculiar offshoot from Shakespeare's dramatic development. To characterize the drama as a satire on any of his contemporaries' predilections for the classics, or to interpret it
as a contribution to the theatrical war is as misleading as to interpret it as a contribution to comical satire, or as an expression
of the author's disillusionment over chivalry, love, life, etc. To
see the significance of the play in any of these conceptions is to
fail to see it in the context of the plays that precede or follow,

11. G. L. Kittredge, The Complete Works of Shakespeare (Boston,
1936), p. 880.
1. Theodore Spencer, Shakespeare and the Nature of Man (New
York, 1943); E. M. W. Tillyard, The Elizabethan World Picture
(New York, 1944); Una Ellis-Fermor, The Frontiers of Drama
(London, 1945).

and Shakespeare's development is too organic to permit an offshoot, an eccentricity.

Neither in Hamlet, in which a young man's disillusionment is
the essence of the tragedy, nor in the tragedies that precede Hamlet,
is a destructive passion pointed up as the essence of tragedy. But
passions baneiul to the possessors are exemplified in the stories
of the three warriors in Troilus and Cressida. Achilles is the
first of Shakespeare's principal tragic heroes afflicted grievously
by passions. He is harmed, and because of his position in society,
the society as a whole is affected.

Shakespeare stresses Achilles' pride with an insistence which
shows that the dramatist was pre-occupied with it and its tragic
potentialities, though it is not only pride he suffers from. In the
Iliades, however, Achilles is justified in his withdrawal, even
though the consequences are deplored, because of the affront Agamemnon has dealt his honor. But Shakespeare omitted the honorable
reason for his withdrawal, and has attributed it essentially to too
much pride. Though such an alteration obscures Homer's conception, the change illuminates Shakespeare's interest in the character, and clearly indicates the dramatist's purpose—the examination
and effect of the passion itself on the possessor. Achilles' pride
so blinds him that he will give up fame and honor, and not care a
jot if the expedition founders. However, Achilles is not the only
character afflicted by passion. Hector, for personal glory, ignores
the urgent demands of the laws of society, nations, and nature.
His renown is worth more than the life of Ilium. And Troilus'
judgment is not so distinguished as his ardor. In council as in love,
his nature leads him to folly. So Othello, Lear, Macbeth, Corio-
lanus, and Antony, in different ways, are subject to an overgrowth
of a faculty that wrecks their judgments and indirectly the societies
about them. Achilles, as he appears in Chapman and Shakespeare,
is kith and kin to them, though his story is different. So also are
Troilus and Hector "relatives."

Troilus and Cressida may be regarded as the gateway to the
later tragedies. To consider it, however, as a problem play, or
dark comedy, or comical satire, is to remove this extraordinarily
rich, and fascinating play from the current of Shakespeare's developing dramaturgy.

APPENDIXES

APPENDIXES

I. *Incidents in Lydgate's Troy Book*

i

The Siege and Withdrawal of Achilles.—The situation Lydgate describes is the same as that in Caxton. Their versions have no connection with Shakespeare's [Troy Book, III.3554 ff.].

ii

In Lydgate's version of the embassy, Agamemnon, leader of the host, sends Ulysses, Diomedes, and Nestor to entreat Achilles to stop the bloodshed of the Greeks by taking part in the battles. Achilles receives the legates with "digne reuerence and with right knightly chere." Ulysses is the only member of the group to speak. He does so at considerable length. He reminds Achilles of that time some years ago when he was most eager to undertake the expedition against Priam and his folk. Now he allows his former desires, which brought him present fame, to relapse. Until now Fortune has favored him:

> . . . youre highe renoun
> Atteyned hath the exaltacioun
> And highest prikke of Fortunys whele,
> It were gret wronge, and ye loke wele,
> Of wilfulnes for to ben vnkynde
> To hir that ye so frendly to you fynde,
> . . . .
> Wherfore, allas, whi wil ye suffer passe
> Youre noble fame, of verray wilfulnes,
> While it is hiest in his worthiness?
> [Troy Book, IV. 1749 ff.]

By this time Achilles has lost his "reuerence and right knightly chere." He replies that the war has accomplished only one purpose. It has drawn off the best blood in the world which will now be possessed by "rural folke and cherles eke." Achilles will not risk his life again, not even for renown.

> For worthines, after deth I-blowe,
> Is but a wynde, & lasteth but a throwe;

145

> For though renoun & pris be blowe wyde,
> Foryetilnes leith it ofte a-syde
> By lengthe of yeris and obliuioun,
> Thorugh envie and fals collucioun.   [IV. 1871 ff.]

When they have stated their case, and Achilles his, the legates
return to Agamemnon.

iii

In Lydgate's version of the Trojan war, the battle between Ajax
and Hector takes place at an early date in the war, soon after the
Greeks have gained a foothold on the Trojan plain [Troy Book, III.
2036 ff.]. The combat itself does not result from a challenge. The
meeting between the cousins in the press is, in Lydgate's words,
casual; its consequences, however, are dire.

> For, as he rood, this Hector, cruelly
> Amonge Grekis slowe and bar al doun,—
> Casuely he meete Thelamoun
> I mene Aiax, nyghe of all allye,
> That of hate and cruel hoot envie
> To Hector rood, like as he were wood,
> Al-be to hym he was [ful] nyghe of blod; [III. 2036 ff.]

Lydgate makes more than Caxton of the fierceness of the combat,
and of the fury with which the contestants engage one another. His
description does not suggest "a maiden battle."

> And this Aiax . . .
> Sette on Hector, of knyghtly highe prowes;
> And, as they mette, both in her wodnes,
> On her stedis, this manly champiouns,
> Eueryche on other lik tigers or lyons
> Be-gan to falle, and proudly to assaille,
> And furiously seuere plate and maille,—
> First with speris, longe, large, & rounde,
> And aftirwarde with swerdis kene grounde:
> [III. 2049 ff.]

When Hector recognizes Ajax as his cousin, he ceases fighting,
and attempts to prevail on Ajax, since he is part Trojan, to leave
the Greek force and visit his relatives in Troy. But Ajax, whatever his lineage, is a Greek by birth, and Greek in upbringing,
and he refuses to go with Hector.

> That sithen he of berthe was a Greke,
> And was of youthe amonge hem fostered eke
> From the tyme of his natiuite,
> And taken had the ordre and degre
> Of knyghthood eke amongis hem a-forn,
> And, ouer this, bounde was and sworn
> To be trewe to her nacioun,
> Making of blood noon excepcioun,
> He swore he wolde conserven his biheste;
> [III. 2097 ff.]

Ajax, though he cannot accept Hector's request, has one of his
own to make.

> That yif that he [Hector] of manful gentilnes,
> Wolde of knyghthood and of worthines
> Shewe vn-to hym so gret affeccioun,
> To make hem that wer of Troye toun
> Only with-drawe Grekis to pursewe,
> And fro her tentis make hem to remewe,
> And resorte ageyn vn-to the toun,
> Of knyghtly routhe and compassioun,
> With-oute assailyng, or any more affray
> Made on Grekis for that ilke day . . . .   [III.2107 ff.]

Hector unwisely grants Ajax's request, and thereby seals the
doom of Troy.

> For fro that day, fare-wel for euere-more
> Victorie & laude fro hem of the toun,
> To hem denyed by disposicioun
> Of mortal fate, whiche was contrarie . . . .
>   [III.2148 ff.]

iv

During one of the many truces in the Trojan war, Hector "in
herte caughte an appetitie" [III.3762], "Whan agreeable was the
morwe gray, Blaundiss(h)inge and plesant of delit," to visit the
enemy in his own camp [III.3764 ff.]. "With many worthi in his
company" [III.3766], he went first to the tent of Achilles, who
had great desire in his heart "bothe day and nyght, Of worthi
Hector for to han a sight" [III.3733—34].

> For neuer his lyue, by non occasioun
> He myght of hym han non inspeccioun,
> Nor hym be-holde at good liberte;
> For vnarmed he myght him neuer se.   [III.3775 ff.]

Achilles informs Hector in no uncertain terms, even though he
is his guest, that he intends to kill him, to avenge the many wounds
inflicted on his flesh [III.3796 ff.], and above all to revenge Patroclus' death, which he will never forgive and can never forget
[III.3823 ff.].

Hector, of course, promises a similar fate to Achilles. But
to prevent the slaughter that time has in store for Trojans and
Greeks alike, Hector proposes to Achilles that between them they
decide the fate of Troy by a personal conflict [III.2823 ff.]. In
agreement, Achilles "caste a gloue doun, In signe & tokene of
confirmacioun, For lyfe or deth that the wil holde his day Ageyn
Hector" [III.4029—32]. Inopportunely for them, Agamemnon, with
his councilors, arrives at Achilles' tent and refuses to trust the
outcome of the war to the efforts of one man.

v

In the <u>Troy Book</u>, Andromache's dream represents Hector's
fate before it is fulfilled.

> Hir thought[e] pleynly, yif the next[e] day
> Hector went his fomen for to assaille,
> As he was wont, armyd in bataille,
> That he ne shulde eskapen outterly,
> In fatis hondis to falle finally;   [III.4918 ff.]

Andromache's dream is Hector's good angel in disguise: but he
sees in it only dubious conclusions that fantastic people draw:

> Where-of, God wote, he toke litel hede,
> But ther-of hadde indignacioun,
> Platly affermyng, that no discrecioun
> Was to trest in swiche fantasies,
> In dremys shewid, gladly meynt with lyes,
> Ful of iapis and illusiouns,
> Of whiche, pleynly, the conclusiouns
> Be nat ellis but folkis to delude . . . .   [III.4942 ff.]

Andromache, unable to persuade her husband, seeks Priam who
is able to restrain Hector, although not his wrath which rises
against his wife.

> . . . of highe dispit he brent,
> Whan that he saw other lordis went
> Oute at the gate, and he alone abood;
> For whiche he wexe furious & wood,
> Hooly the cause arrettynge to his wif . . . .
>   [III.5027 ff.]

As in the <u>Recuyell</u>, Hector returns to combat when his bastard
brother is slain by Achilles.

vi

"Nighe al this yere," the Greeks, according to Diomedes, idled
away time sacking towns and amassing spoils at Tenedos, and
making minor expeditions in the surrounding regions, while the
great purpose of the expedition remained forgotten [II.7941 ff.].
Believing his advice to get on with the siege of Troy quite sensible,
the Greeks set sail, and by the evening of that day establish their
camp, after considerable fighting, on the Trojan coast. On the
next morning, when "the rowes rede Of Phebus chare gonne for
to sprede" [II.8701-2], Hector draws up his battalions in Troy,
while Agamemnon marshals his host below the citadel.

> And of the first [battalion] he yaf gouernaunce
> To the manful noble Patroclus
> That with hym ladde (myn auctour telleth thus)
> Miundones, so myghti and so stronge,
> With alle the folke that to Achilles longe . . .
> . . . .
> Nowe, fille it so on the same day

> That Achilles kepte hym in his tente,
> And for seknes that day oute ne wente;
> For his lechis made hym to abstene,
> For his woundes fresche wern & grene
> That ke kaught on the day to-fore . . . . [III.576 ff.]

On the same day, and the day after the Greeks first landed on the plain, Patroclus rode into battle against Hector when "he him saw a-fer" [III.761]. But the encounter proved disastrous.

> This myghti man, this Troyan champioun,
> In his Ire ay brennynge more and more,
> Vp-on hym the hate frat so sore,
> Lefte his spere, myn auctor writeth thus,
> And with a swerd rood to Patroclus,
> Avised fully that he schal be ded;
> And furiously gan hamen at his hed,
> And rof hym doun, ther was no maner lette,
> In-to the brest thorugh his basenet,
> As seith Guydo, with so gret a peyne,
> That with the stroke he partid hym on tweyne.
>   [III.778 ff.]

vii

Achilles was "smyte with Cupidys darte" on the anniversary of Hector's death, on the day he saw Polyxena among the group of Trojan women that was attending service in the temple of Apollo. To assuage his passion, which increases as soon as he returns to his tent, Achilles proposes to King Priam, through a a messenger, that in return for his daughter as wife, he will achieve a peace between the Greek and Trojan forces. Priam is not averse to the idea.

> And for to saue myn other sonys alle,
> I will concent that this Achilles,
> So that he make a trewe final pes
> Atwene Grekis and also this cite,
> With-oute more, pleinly, how that he
> Haue vn-to wyfe my doughter Polycene. [IV. 868 ff.]

Achilles cannot persuade the Greeks that there is an advantage in peace. To leave in peace a city they are besieging in hate is not their policy. Achilles, however, sees no loss of honor in withdrawing from Troy and leaving it to the Trojans. The Greeks still possess Hesione.

> But list some man wil make obieccioun
> That we may nat [so] our honoure saue,
> To repeire, pleynly, but we haue
> Eleyne ageyn, that is cause of al:—
> To whiche thing anoon answer I shal,
> Yif any man in his fantasie,
> To dishonour or to vyllanye
> Arrette wolde, in any maner kynde,

We to gon hom & leven hir be-hynde,
Shortly to seyn, I holde it be no shame,
Sith that we han on as gret of name . . . .[IV. 1110 ff.]

viii

In Lydgate's history of the siege, Patroclus' death does not
stir Achilles to take instant action against Hector. A considerable
interval of time elapses between Patroclus' death and Hector's.
Achilles never forgets Patroclus, but it is not the powerful motive
for instant action that it is in Troilus and Cressida and in the Iliades.

And of o thing moste is my greuaunce,
Whan I haue fully remembraunce,

. . . .

How thou madist a diuisioun
Of me, allas! and of Patroclus,
So yonge, so manly, and so vertuous!   [III.3823 ff.]

Achilles slays Hector only when he gets the chance. That opportunity does not offer itself until long after Patroclus has been slain.
Achilles' withdrawal takes place on the anniversary of Hector's
death. The slaughter of the Myrmidons, and the armed attack of
50,000 Trojans, compel him to leave his retreat and to take up
arms to save his life. Troilus like a "wood lyon" is mostly responsible for the defeat of the Myrmidons.

And somme he smet euene thorugh the syde,
Thorugh the body, & some thorugh the herte;

. . . .

He slow that day of hem many oon,
That maugre hem thei fledden euerychon,
With the Grekis, eueryche to his tent.   [IV. 2480 ff.]

An unidentified Greek warns Achilles to arm.

"Allas", quod he, "how may ye sustene
To sen your men her vp-on the grene
A-fore youre face slayn & ly[e] dede,
And liste nat onys for to taken hede,
But stonde stille, pensif in youre tent,
Vp-on the point youre silfe to be shent
In hasty hour, yif ye here abide:
For fifty thousand knyghtes here be-side,
Redy armyd in platis and in maille,
Cast hem pleinly attonys you tassaille" —

. . . .

This Achilles, like as he were wood,
Armyd hym, fomynge as a boor;—   [IV. 2525 ff.]

and in a short time, he dispatches Troilus.

ix

Agamemnon summons his councilors to devise a plan to slay

Hector, since the Greeks are unable in fair and open fight to bring about his death. Achilles, above all others, is selected as most fit to execute the plan.

> And whan thei wern assemblid alle y-fere,
> . . . thei gan to conspire blive
> The deth of hym, in many sondry woye,
> Echon concludynge, while he wer in Troy
> It was nat likly Grekis for to wynne;
> . . . .
> Thei condiscende to this conclusioun:
> That be som sleight of a-wait lying,
> Whan he were most besy in fightynge,
> Amongis hem in meschef or distresse,
> That Achilles do his besynes,
> With al his myght vnwarly him to assaille,
> That hym to slen for no thing that he faille.
> And Grekis alle gan her prayer make
> To Achilles for to vndirtake
> Of this emprise fynally the swt,
> Thorugh his manhod that it be execut—   [III. 2685 ff.]

The opportunity presents itself when Achilles sees Hector stripping a corpse of its armour.

> Reklesly, the story maketh mynde,
> He cast his shelde at his bak be-hynde,
> To welde hym silf at more liberte,
> And for to han opportunyte
> To spoillen hym, and for mo wyght spare,
> So that his brest disarmyd was & bare:
> Except his platis ther was no diffence
> Ageyn the strok to make resistence.   [III. 5375 ff.]

Achilles, "cruel and venemous"

> Of hertly hate most malencolyous,—
> Whiche couertly havynge hym be-side,
> Whan that he saw Hector disarmyd ride,
> He hent a spere, sharpe grounde & kene,
> And of Ire in his hateful tene,
> All vnwarly, or Hector myghte aduerte,
> (Allas the whyle!) he smote hym to the herte,
> Thorugh-oute the brest, that ded he fil doun
> Vn-to the erthe, this Troyan champioun,
> Thorough necligence only of his shelde! [III. 5390 ff.]

When Hector is slain,

> Thei of Troye, with great reuerence
> Dide her labour and her dilligence
> The ded cors to carien in-to toun
> Of worthi Hector, whan Titan went[e] doun.
>   [III. 5413 ff.]

x

As in the <u>Recuyell</u>, the meeting of the Trojan councilors in
the <u>Troy Book</u> takes place before the Ten Years' War begins.
Priam summons his council to inform the peers and "commons"
of Troy of his desire to send an expedition to Greece, to ravage
it as Troy was twice ravaged, and, if possible, to free Hesione
from her present bondage. Above all, he begs Hector to support
his will.

Hector declares that no man is more conscious than he of the
necessity of righting a wrong. The law of nature demands that
past injuries be atoned for.

> After the force and the grete myght,
> And the somme of naturis right
> Which euery thing by kynde doth constreyne
> In the boundis of hir large cheyne,
> It fittyng is, as sche doth enspire,
> And acordyng that euery man desyre
> Of wrongis don to han amendement,
> And to hir law right conuenient . . . .   [II.2185 ff.]

It is the bounden duty of a noble man, above all others, to perform this obligation.

> Only of knyghthod oure worschip for to eke,
> Of wrongis don amendis for to seke,
> Oure staat consydered & oure highe noblesse,
> And in what plyte we stonde of worthines,
> Whan that bestis, of resoun rude and blinde,
> Desire the same by instynt of kynde.   [II.2211 ff.]

But, on the other hand, not to weigh the consequences that the
revenge may provoke is to act without judgment. Who knows
what will follow an aggressive policy?

> But first I rede, wysely in your minde
> To cast aforn and leue nat be-hynde
> Or ye be-gynne . . .
> Al, only nat the gynnyng but the ende,
> And the myddes, what weie thei wil wende,
> And to what fyn Fortune wil hem lede—   [II.2229 ff.]

Hector calls Priam's attention to the wide empire the Greeks
control, to the great number of hardy knights they can assemble
to revenge any wrong. Furthermore, Hesione is old, and may
not live long. She is not worth the gamble.

Paris is not content with Hector's cautious approach to the
problem. He begs Priam to send him into Greece, and give him
a chance to fulfill the prophecy embodied in his dream.

Deiphobus supports Paris. Hector is too cautious. If a man
considers the end of an enterprise before he undertakes it, there
will be no venturing.

> . . . yif that euery wight
> Aduerten schuld & castyn in his sight
> Of future thing the pereil & the doute,
> And cerchyn it with-Innen & with-oute,
> . . . .
> Thanne no wyght schulde to no purpos wende
> In any mater for to make an ende,
> Or dar presvme by manhod in his thought.
> [II.2847 ff.]

The council is suddenly abashed by Helenus' warning that if Paris goes, Troy will fall [II.2985 ff.]. Troilus, however, soon rouses the council from dejection.

> What sodeyn fere hath brought you in this rage?
> What new[e] trouble is cropen in your brest,
> For the sentence of a cowarde prest?—
> Sith thei echon, as ye schal euer fynde,
> Desyre more, verrayly, of kynde,
> To lyue in lust & voide awey traueyle,
> And dedly hate to heren of bataille . . . . [II.3004 ff.]

During the siege itself, Priam summons his council to pass on the Greek demand for a truce. Hector opposes this request, for what the Greeks really want is time to re-supply and re-victual their army. When Hector sees that the councilors are in favor of granting the truce, he withdraws his objection.

> Yit neuertheles, how-euere that it be,
> Towchyng this trew for monthes thre,
> Sethen ye alle assenten and accorde,
> Fro youre sentence I wil nat discorde,
> In no wyse to be variaunt. [III.3653 ff.]

The author then laments Priam's decision:

> Whi hast thou sauour in bitter more than swete,
> That canst nat lyue in pes nor in quyete?
> Thou art travailed with wilful mocions,
> Ouermaystred with thi passiouns,
> For lak of resoun and of highe prudence,
> Dirked & blind . . . . [II.1807–12]

II. Lydgate's Fall of Princes

In the Fall of Princes, Lydgate covers the history of the Trojan wars with unexpected dispatch—in about seven stanzas [John Lydgate, Fall of Princes, ed. Henry Bergen (E.E.T.S., London, 1924), I.i.5986–6035]. The ancient story is a prime example of what unstable Fortune does to persons in high places. Those who have pride in temporal power, and who are primarily concerned with worldly joy, are most subject to misfortune.

Ye proude folkis that sette your affiaunce
In strengthe, beute or in hih noblesse,
Yff ye considre Fortunys variaunce,
And coude a merour affor your eyen dresse
Off kyng Priam and off his gret richesse,
To seen how he and [how] his children all
From ther noblesse so sodenli befall!

Ector off knyhthod callid sours and well,
Sad and demur & famous off prudence,
Paris also in beute dede excell,
And Helenus in parfit prouidence;
Troilus in armys hadde gret experience,
Eek Deiphebus preued manli on his fon:
Yit in the werre thei wer slayn euerichon.

· ·

Whan that he [Priam] sat hiest on hir wheel,
This blynde goddesse gan hym to assaile.

· ·

By which exaumple all proude men may see
The onseur trust, the mutabilite,

Which in this world is seyn & found alday. [I.i.6042 ff.]

From time to time in the <u>Fall</u>, Lydgate returns to the story
of the siege to narrate some particular event to illustrate his
thesis. Pride and adultery caused the war, and brought destruction to Trojans and Greeks alike.

For thauoutrie off Paris and Heleyne
Brouhte al Troye to destruccioun;
Pride & luxure were also menys tweyne
Whi Grekis leide a siege to the toun,
And fynal cause off ther confusioun,
To outher parti losse of many a man,
The ground conceyued whi first the werre gan.

This tragedie pitous & lamentable
And dolerous to writen & expresse,
That worthi Priam, of kynges most notable,
Was falle in pouert from his gret richesse,
Fro kyngli honour into wrechidnesse,
Fro sceptre & crowne, & from his regalie
To myschieff brouht thoruh fals auoutrie.

Was nat Fortune froward and deceyuable
For to suffre bi her doubilnesse,
And bi hir cours, which euer is variable,
That worthi Ector, flour off hih prowesse,
Sholde onwarli, most famous off noblesse,
Be slayn allas, cheef stok off chiualrie,
For a quarell off fals auoutrie?			[I.i.6301 ff.]

If Shakespeare had recourse to the <u>Fall</u> while writing his play,
he left no evidence in the drama of a specific debt to incidents in

the poem. Those portions that deal with the body of material
Shakespeare used in the drama are too general to have been useful
to him in constructing his plot.

III.*Peele's Tale of Troy*

George Peele, in The Tale of Troy, first published in 1589,
covers those years of Trojan history between the birth of Paris
and the death of Hecuba. For the most part, Peele treats the
separate incidents that make up the Trojan saga so briefly that
they are not of much help to the dramatist who needs details to
build up a dramatic situation. Furthermore, most of the material
treated in the poem lies too far outside Shakespeare's nucleus
of action to prove useful to him. What parallel action there is in
the Tale of Troy is probably fortuitous.

After Paris has escaped with Helen the vigilance of the Spartan
guards, and the chances of arresting the flight are dim, Menelaus
and the Greeks assemble to force Priam to return the Spartan
queen. The fleet is becalmed at Aulis, until Agamemnon appeases
Artemis.

> The flower of Greece and armies all by this,
> For want of wind, had hover'd long in Aulis:
> . . . .
> Away they fly, their tackling toft and tight,
> As shoots a streaming star in winter's night;
> A thousand ships well-rigg'd, a glorious sight,
> Waving ten thousand flags, they leave the port;
> And, as ye wot, this war and tragic sport
> It was for Helena[1]. . . .

The traditional embassy Ulysses makes to Priam's court, in
an attempt to win Helen back by peaceful means, is not an incident
that is mentioned by Peele, and only by indirect reference does
Shakespeare show his familiarity with it [Troilus and Cressida,
IV. i.1 ff.]. The meeting of the Trojan council, however, which
Shakespeare developed into a lengthy scene, is mentioned by Peele
in a few lines.

> The King of Troy gan quickly understand
> How Greeks with all their power were hard at hand;
> And sadly do the peers their prince advise,
> The while in rage Cassandra calls and cries,
> "Render, ye Trojans, to these madding Greeks
> The dame that all this expedition seeks." [p. 555]

1. The Dramatic and Poetic Works of Robert Greene and George
Peele, ed. Alexander Dyce (London, 1861), p. 554.

The chivalric character of the engagements is emphasized by
Peele in his descriptions of the encounters between warriors:

> How many Greeks, how many Trojan knights,
> As chivalry by kind in love delights,
> Upon their helmets can their plumes advance,
> And twist their ladies' colours on their lance.
> So doth this love make men adventurous:
> So hardy was the true knight Troilus,
> And all for love of the unconstant Cressed,
>
> . . . .
>
> And that I may give every man his right,
> Sir Paris mounted, in his armour bright,
> Pricks forth, and on his helm his mistress'
>   sleeve:
> How could that sight but Menelaus grieve?   [p. 555]

Achilles, the fiercest of the Greeks, is fast enthralled by
Polyxena.

> The time of truce set down by martial law,
> The dame of Troy with lovely looks do draw
> The hearts of many Greeks, and, lo, at last,
> The great Achilles is enthralled fast,
> That night ne day he might his rest enjoy;
> So was his heart engagèd whole to Troy,
> Thàt now no more of arms this warrior would,
> Or, mought I say, no more for love he could:
> The camp complains upon his love and sloth,
> And charge him with his knighthood and his oath.
> Now rides out Hector, call'd the scourge of Greeks,
> And, like the untam'd panther, pries and seeks
> Where he may prove his strength; and, storming thus,
> He lights upon Achilles' friend, Patroclus.
> King Peleus' son, thus rous'd, soon gan him greet,
> And, lion-like, runs fiercely him to meet,
> For rescue of his friend, as he were wood,
> And charging so his staff in furious mood,
> As falcon wants to stoop upon his prey,
> Forgetful of the fair Polyxena,
> As Hector has unhors'd Patroclus tho,
> Despoiling him in field, the more the woe,
> Unwares to wreak Patroclus' death beleek,
> He slays a peerless Trojan for a Greek;
> And having thus perform'd this piece of treason,
> He triumphs in the spoils of Priam's son.   [p. 555]

It should be observed that in the poem and in the play Achilles
falls in love with Polyxena before Hector is slain, and also before
Patroclus is slain. As far as I know this parallel between the poem
and the play is shared by few accounts of the story written definitely before 1602. In the Recuyell and the Troy Book, Achilles
falls in love with Polyxena on the first anniversary of Hector's

death, and many years after Patroclus'. The swift climax that
Peele describes is duplicated by the action of the play, though one
is not therefore to suppose that Shakespeare was dependent on
Peele. Since the dramatist felt obliged to include the Achilles-
Polyxena episode within the limits of the plot, there was no other
conceivable place in the drama to which he could allocate the
episode without totally destroying the unity of action. To place
the Achilles-Polyxena episode in its traditional place, Shakespeare would have had to follow the Caxton sequence of events,
and then he would have had a chronicle rather than a drama
shaping up, and not the drama he purposely fashioned from the
Homeric sequence of events, and into the frame of which he introduced incidents from the Recuyell.

The rest of the poem deals with the deaths of Achilles, Ajax,
Priam, and Hecuba, and the general destruction of Troy, which
were events of no concern to Shakespeare.

INDEX OF PASSAGES CITED

INDEX OF PASSAGES CITED